WOMEN THRIVE

INSPIRING TRUE STORIES OF WOMEN OVERCOMING ADVERSITY

RAIMONDA JANKUNAITE   DEEPIKA SANDHU

VICKY MIDWOOD   NEETU DEOL JHAJ

ANGELIC INGRAM   MARY GOUGANOVSKI

ERICA TATUM-SHEADE   DR. COYLETTE JAMES

DEDICATION

This book is dedicated to you, the woman who aspires for more in life. A woman who knows that despite your pains and struggles, you are meant for more. A woman who wants to thrive and is inspired by other women rising to their power and purpose in life.

For a woman who wants to become aligned, live a purposeful life and create the freedom to be who she was created to be. Be unapologetically you.

"A butterfly cannot see its wings, but the rest of us can. Remember: you are beautiful, and while you may not see it, we can."

Do you feel inspired to share highlights of this book on social media? We would love for you to use hashtag #WomenThriveBook and tag us @womenthrivemedia

To get to know our authors and to get access to special gifts from each author, please visit www.womenthrivesummit.com/book .

CONTENTS

WHY THIS BOOK EXISTS

At Women Thrive Media, our mission is to create a stage where every woman can have the opportunity to shine. A place where she can share her story and, by doing so, inspire others.

Over the years, we have met thousands of women through in-person and virtual events, and our community and every woman had a story to share. In our work, we have had the opportunity to spotlight close to a thousand women across our event stages and podcast; however, there is much more to do.

This book is the first of many - because writing your story in a book is so much more magical and personal than simply speaking; the words we write on paper live on forever. We hope this book finds space on your bookshelf, coffee table, or library alongside other inspirational books.

The process of writing your story is healing and liberating. It is healing and liberating for the readers and the authors themselves. We learned that the process of writing your story could become a transformation in itself and create so many opportunities for growth.

Through our Women Thrive book series, we hope to give as many women as possible the opportunity to write their stories in a book and inspire the world with words of encouragement. Sharing stories of overcoming adversities in life and finding the way forward to rise and thrive.

If you would like to contribute to our future Women Thrive Book series, please visit www.womenthrivesummit.com/book, where you will find our interest form.

On our website, you will also find video interviews with every speaker from the Women Thrive Podcast, or you can also find us on most podcast streaming platforms by searching Women Thrive. This is a fantastic opportunity to get to know our speakers and hear more about their journeys as an author in this book.

INTRODUCTION

Dear reader,

As you read this book, I hope you take a moment to immerse yourself in every story written on these pages, as every chapter in this book was written for you to help you thrive.

This book has been written by eight amazing women from different parts of the world, backgrounds and life experiences. Before this project, they had never met each other before, but they all shared something in common: a mission to positively impact others through the power of their stories. Some of these women have never shared these powerful stories before, so this is a very intimate experience for them to pour their hearts out to you, the reader, in hopes that it will make a difference in your life. Sharing our stories of overcoming adversities and some of the darkest moments of our lives is not easy. It takes a lot of courage, soul searching, self-questioning, doubting and, in the end, bravery to speak our truth. To lay our adversities bare on the line for someone else to read and experience it requires re-living our stories and doing a lot of inner healing.

You may not resonate with all these stories today, but the story that touches you the least today may be just what you need to hear down the road. May one of these stories impact your life just when you need it the most. The purpose of this book is to inspire you, the reader, to know that life comes with adversities, unexpected twists and turns, moments when you seem to have it all, and life just pulls the rug from under your feet, we hope that this book inspires you to keep going despite those life challenges. For some, the start in life was not as fortunate, and some of these women could have ended up as a tragedy. For others, adversities happened later in life, which taught them valuable lessons and helped them find the purpose in their pain.

These authors have experienced some truly trying times that nearly broke them, but in those moments of defeat, they found strength, courage, awakening and renewed purpose. These women share their stories in hopes that you won't have to feel alone in your struggles and that you may find courage and inspiration in their bravery.

As you read the pages of this book, remember that this could be someone's survival guide. Please share it with someone else, recommend it to your friends, leave a review, or send a thank you note to the author whose chapter inspired you. I promise you that is the most rewarding part of writing a book: hearing from our readers and how our message has impacted them. It is the biggest blessing and gift to have our stories out in the world, touching people's lives.

As you pick up the book the picture on the cover may remind you of the different phases of life, and different moments of transformation. There may be one face that particularly stands out for you today, and another the next time you hold this book in your hands. This book is meant to be an inspirational journey, an experience where every time you read it there may be something new you will discover, about the author, their story or about yourself. As you go through your life's journey, you may face similar challenges, or may have already had to overcome your own trials, and found inspiration and courage to move through them. May this book be a reminder of just how strong, resilient, and capable we all are of overcoming adversities and finding the way through them to thrive.

Raimonda Jankunaite

STARTING A NEW CHAPTER

By Raimonda Jankunaite

There is something really empowering about looking in the car's rear view mirror and seeing all your belongings in the back of the car, knowing a new chapter of your life is about to begin.

It was June 2021. I had made the pivotal decision to leave everything I had built for the last six years with a man I loved. To pack my stuff and walk out to start a new life.

As I drove away from my home on that warm, sunny day, I felt a sudden release: from here on out, I was in control of my own life and my destiny.

I didn't have it all figured out, far from it. I just had to trust in the path yet to unfold that it would become better the further I walked into it. I didn't have a place to live, nothing to call my own except my clothes and a few belongings I had taken with me. I didn't know how I would manage on my own, and I just had to have faith that all would work out.

As I was driving away, my phone rang. It was one of my business friends, with whom I had chatted just a few days ago, about the messy divorce she was going through with her narcissistic husband. Just a few days ago, I was giving her advice on how to handle the situation she was navigating with her abusive and possessive ex, blissfully unaware that I would soon be in the same position.

As I picked up the phone, we greeted each other, and she said, "Wait - why do you have all these things in the back of your car? Where are you going?"

I smiled and said, "I have something to tell you: I AM ON MY WAY TO START A NEW LIFE!"

I was beaming with a smile and felt more empowered than ever before. Not because it didn't hurt but because I knew I deserved better than the lies and deceit I lived in.

As she looked at me - she said, "It looks like you are the energy that is moving the car, not the other way around." It was true - the car was filled with my stuff and a newfound empowerment that was moving the vehicle forward. My energy was: "LIFE, I AM READY FOR YOU!"

She said, "I wish I were as strong and determined when I left my husband; I was a total wreck."

I wasn't a wreck because I was relieved to make the escape that I did, not realising that the wreck would come further down the line, filled with pain, anger, tears, frustration and much more.

It was all about that moment, the sudden realisation that this decision was much bigger than me and my life. I told her that I made this leap not just for myself but for all the other women who may be stuck in a hopeless situation at home. For women who have given their power away for love and succumbed to lies, control and deceit. For women who don't yet see that a better life is laid out for them, if only they dare to leap. For all the women who deserve better.

Travelling in the Wrong Direction

A few months before this happened, it was a pretty ordinary weekend at home. As always, I was home alone because my partner had other commitments every weekend. I remember walking into our bedroom, looking at the sun beaming on the perfectly made bed, my favourite picture on the wall, and a dark wooden chest of draws with little crystals laid out on the top. It was a peaceful and quiet afternoon.

In the room were our happy memories. Our smiling pictures hung by the bed in heart-shaped frames from our highlight moments. It all looked perfect on the outside. We didn't lack anything, we weren't arguing, and there was no real issue that felt prominent except the underlying feeling that something was wrong, so at that moment, I had an awakening vision.

I could only describe this vision like my life was moving on a parallel road to the one I was meant to live in. As if I knew that this was not my road to be on anymore, and the longer I stayed on it, the further away I was moving from my purpose. I knew there was nothing else I could do on this path right here that would lead me to where I was supposed to be.

I felt sadness. Inside I felt empty, as one too many shattered dreams and plans never came to fruition, making me feel hopeless in the situation I was in. There were too many disappointments and things that did not make sense, but I was still there, hoping it would change. Time and time again, I was compromising and finding excuses for someone else, yet suffering inside myself, putting my dreams on hold, and playing the waiting game. I was waiting for something big to happen, to either make or break our relationship.

It was never the right time to make changes to the life that we both supposedly wanted. It was never the right time to move, travel, start something new or take a leap towards our goals and dreams. There was always a convenient excuse or a reason why not now.

Have you ever felt like your life was moving in a particular direction and you felt like hitting the brakes and saying: "I need to get out."? Or feeling so stagnant that you are just watching the clock tick and your life's destiny run away from you?

Tick tock, tick tick, how long are you going to wait? What needs to happen for you to hit the brakes and restart your life again?

Maybe in your life, it's a job that feels stale and unfulfilling; perhaps it's a relationship that no longer feels right for you; maybe it's a business that you've been stuck with, and it feels out of alignment.

However, you continue going through your daily motions, hoping for something big to happen to change. Still, over and over again, you are experiencing the same feeling of being on the wrong side of the motorway just as I was, travelling in the wrong direction.

That was my life - I wanted to hit the brakes - but it seemed like I travelled this far - maybe there is still hope at the end of it all? Perhaps somehow, we will still reach our destination? I know; that was my wishful thinking as a perpetual optimist.

The further I moved, the more I realised that this was not the road I should remain on. Whilst the road I was on did not lack mutual love, support and material things, it lacked an open and honest truth and commitment. It was built on control, manipulation and selective truth to keep me at bay. After six years of living together, there was simply no progress in our life, and I was at a crossroads.

At that moment, I knew even if tomorrow everything in our current situation changed to how I dreamed that one day it would be - I knew it would be just a matter of time before the bubble burst and everything would fall apart.

In Control of Your Own Destiny

I realised that if I wanted anything to change, I had to take a leap of faith. No matter how uncertain, scary and uncomfortable it felt, I had to put a hard stop to my life as I knew it and start again. I knew there would be no easy way to do it, and it just had to be done.

Tony Robbins says, "Change happens when the pain of staying the same is greater than the pain of change." This was true for me - because, from the outside, what seemed quite an ordinary and happy life, on the inside, I knew it was no longer in alignment with me. I had to stop fooling myself and recognise that I was the only one in control of my life. As much as I could blame others for not moving or changing to my expectations, I had to become the driver of my destiny.

I realised that over the years, I had changed so much from the inside out that the life I had built no longer made sense. I was not willing to sacrifice any more, and I was not willing to stay quiet and accept our reality for what it was. I was no longer willing to put up with a life in which I only saw 50% of the truth.

I also realised that not everyone around me had grown along with me but had instead grown apart from me. Again, expecting someone to change just because you changed is like expecting the rest of the world to move in the same direction as you. You have to realise that you have your mission to follow and purpose to fulfil, and not everyone is meant to be part of the next chapter of your journey. I knew that if I wanted to live a life that was honest to myself and aligned with my values and purpose, I had to make the hard decision to cut my losses and make a leap. After all, I knew I did not come this far, only to accept a mediocre life.

Blocking Our Own Blessings

When you live in misalignment, nothing seems to be moving forward, which was the case for me. Nothing I wished, worked for or tried to manifest was moving forward. It didn't matter if I wrote my goals in the diary, put up vision boards, made concrete plans or worked 24-7 for what I wanted. Nothing was working out.

Until that point in my life, I worked hard, probably harder than most people in regular careers. Having chosen to follow the entrepreneurship route and failing a few of my initial business ideas, I had to work twice as hard to prove a point and make it work. I did not have a guaranteed salary since the age of 21, so everything I earned resulted from my work and sheer commitment.

Despite putting in endless hours in my business and investing in growing it, nothing seemed to work. I had built a huge online following, a well-recognised and respected brand, and helped thousands of people along the way, yet I could not make it work financially for myself. It was as if something was blocking my success, and I was giving away all my energy and getting nothing in return.

So I worked on myself, my skills, my mindset, and my limiting beliefs. I hired help, built a team, worked with coaches, and invested in all the programs you can think of. Yet, I was still just breaking even, meaning making just enough to cover the costs of running it all.

The fact was, it was not like I did not know what I was doing. I was helping many others, and my advice would lead them to start and build successful businesses. I had a business degree, strong business and work ethics and the right idea that was getting the attention of my audience. But time and time again, it would fall short of sustaining me, beyond the business.

After I had tried everything, I honestly didn't know what was getting in my way anymore. I had put it down to a money mindset and limiting beliefs, so I did deep hypnosis and inner healing to get past my limiting beliefs, but it was still a struggle.

Whilst I was with my partner, I did not have to worry about paying the bills at home, so I felt safe being taken care of whilst I built my business. I could solely focus on my work and my business. He was supportive of my dreams and always encouraged me to work hard. We always shared work ethics and striving ambition to succeed in life. So it was a comfortable and safe place to be, knowing I did not have to think about how to survive constantly, and living in London is not easy for a single person. Perhaps it was a blessing and a curse. Financial comfort at home was 'safe', but it also did not allow me to succeed independently.

No matter what I did, nothing was moving things forward in my business. Every launch, every event, and every new product would make enough to pay for itself and the team. I was getting frustrated and exhausted to the point where I questioned everything. Should I even carry on? I nearly gave up many times, but something kept saying: don't give up on it all just yet; something better will come out of this.

Again, in that moment of crossroads, I realised I was blocking my blessings. By staying in my situation, I was not allowing a new flow of abundance and blessings to come into my life. Because I had a fear of letting go of the comfort of my home, security and support system, I was living in fear instead of faith and trust. Without knowing for sure, I knew deep down in my gut that I had to let go of everything and surrender to the unknown.

I knew that I would not be able to fly until I was willing to let go of the solid ground beneath my feet. So I did.

I let go of everything holding my life up in my comfort zone and told myself that, no matter what, I GOT THIS. I will figure it out; if not, somehow, the universe will catch me or show me the way.

I know many women stay in toxic environments because of financial security and fear, but this experience taught me that we, as women, are strong and capable enough to figure it all out on our own. When times are tough, we are capable of becoming even stronger to fight for what it is worth.

Don't get me wrong, it was not easy, and at times I wondered, "How am I going to make it?" but the more I leaned into faith and surrender, the more the universe rewarded me. It rewarded me for every bit of patience and trust I had. Whenever I thought I reached the end of the road, the universe would magically open the path forward. So I kept walking in faith.

Finding My Soul's Purpose

Within days of starting a new chapter in my life, I moved to Spain to live with my mum, who had retired there six months prior. I wanted to be as far away from it all as possible. I needed not only a new chapter in my life, I needed to build a whole new life for myself. I had to start from scratch. I had to figure out who I was, what I wanted, and how I would like to build my life forward. It was both a scary and exciting new beginning.

It took me a few months to find my feet and a place where I felt safe to be myself. I must admit I was a hot mess for a few months while navigating the heartbreak, my quest for freedom and adjusting to the new me. I struggled to work, stay focused or feel like myself. I mainly caused chaos and self-sabotage for a few months. I fell out with my family and ran away from anyone who tried to control me. I had to escape, but mainly from myself. So I sought my own place to call home, and the first place I found, I took it.

I started to breathe and relax when I made the leap to move into my own little rented apartment by the beach. I remember walking into this cute, holiday-like apartment decorated with gorgeous beach house decor touches that reminded me that I had finally escaped my monotonous life in London. The lovely sea shells, crystals, coastal pictures on the walls, empty secret message bottles with little fairy lights and other subtle details made it feel like the true magical escape I needed.

My balcony overlooked the seafront, and the sun shone throughout the day on first the front, then the back balcony, where I spent most of my days. The sound of the ocean mixed with seashell decorations made a beautiful sound all day long, reminding me where I was. It soothed my soul and readied me for healing.

I remember waking up every morning to birds chirping outside my window and the sun peeking through the curtains and feeling so grateful for making the decision to leave and start a new life. I would start my day by thanking myself for the decision I made. This is where my new life's journey began. At this little beachfront apartment, in the winter season, when hardly anyone was around. Just me, sunshine, the sound of the waves, meditation, books and my thoughts.

For the next few months, it was a bliss. I would have a morning run by the beach, swim in the cold sea, and meditate in the afternoons. I could finally be present with myself and be in control of my own life. After so many years of being under control, careful watching and constant mind & emotional tampering, this felt like a breath of fresh air. For someone who is highly independent and, at times, an introverted person, it was necessary for my healing and self-re-discovery journey.

All I needed was solitude to process all that had happened and heal from everything that had gone on before, during, and after my breakup. I also needed to recover what was deeper beneath the surface and find my inner peace again. It was hard at first, as so many conflicting emotions come with it, questioning it all - was it love or a life of deceit? What was the truth and what wasn't. What was love and what was control and emotional manipulation? I could not figure it all out, so I had to accept that some things, I may never know.

I always knew I was passionate about empowering other women and seeing them rise, but only through my own phoenix moment has it become real and purposeful. In some of my messier moments, I've openly shared the experience of this transition with part of my social media audience and friends. Some knew the struggles I was going through in my personal life, but many didn't until I shared it publicly in a moment of despair, when I felt the most vulnerable, isolated and defeated. When everything seemed to have totally crumbled and I was standing on the street in the middle of the night with one suitcase and nowhere to go.

Many reached out to thank me for my bravery in sharing those moments with the world. Because some women too have felt isolated, helpless, stuck and felt like they are alone fighting their battles. Sharing my story of isolation, pain and struggles has helped other women see they are not alone.

Some of the women who reached out to me offered their support and encouragement and stood with me in solidarity when I felt like my whole world turned upside down and against me. In my pain I found my purpose: that I could help others change their lives around, so they too can have the freedom they deserve.

So they can become the best versions of themselves, take ownership of their future and their dreams. It takes a lot of courage to leave life as we know it, especially if we live in fear and the constant message that we would not succeed on our own. The truth is, we are more capable of achieving anything that we set out to do, and the proof lives in me and many other brave women who overcome adversities, and some who shared their stories in this very book as a testimony.

Sharing my story in this book as well as on my social media has been my moment of bravery, now it is your moment to look within and ask yourself - how do you see your life unfolding? Is there something in your life that needs to change in order to align you to your purpose and your truth to set you free?

As I set myself free and started to live my truth, everything started to make sense and one thing after next, the pieces to the puzzle started to fall together. Suddenly my work started to reap rewards more than ever before. I found the right people to help my vision come to life. My audience was truly behind me with my new-found purpose and mission and suddenly it was no longer about me - it became what it was always meant to be: empowering women to rise together and thrive above defeat.

I started to connect with more women who'd been through various adversities in life and we could resonate on a much deeper level and in a profound way that became the secret nod to say: I see you and I understand your pain.

But you don't have to do this on your own. We are all in this together, and we will rise together.

This gave me the strength to share my truth with the world, and continue to do my empowerment and impact work and connect with women worldwide through the power of my story. After I healed and returned to my business a few months later, I received a warm welcome from my audience and it seemed that anything I touched just worked. Suddenly, what I was creating became a movement. I started to connect with women who have also been through similar painful experiences as me, and who had just as powerful stories to share. Women who were just as passionate about positive impact in the world as me.

The Blessings Come When You Least Expect It

When I was going through my pain and healing I could not pretend to be OK, and I did not want to. So I risked losing it all whilst I did my inner work, because I knew my business and my work started with me first and foremost. I felt like I needed that time to heal and find myself first.

As I stepped back into my purpose work after 6 months of healing, I found even more support and encouragement than ever before. The difference was that I felt different about myself, my work, my courage and my purpose. I knew exactly how I wanted my life, my work and my relationships to unfold from there on.

That year, as I opened the doors to our Women Thrive annual women empowerment summit we were flooded with speaker applications and women's interest to participate. I had women from all parts of the world reaching out to me wanting to join our mission.

As I spoke to these women, I discovered that though our backgrounds may be very different, some of the life experiences they have been through are not dissimilar. They, too, have overcome defeat, fear, abuse, tragedy, loss or other life challenges that did not break them, but made them stronger. These women were just as brave, courageous, strong and determined as I was and more than anything, they wanted to share their stories with the world to empower and inspire others.

They inspired me and solidified my mission to build the biggest global community and stage for all women to shine, so every woman's story can be shared globally. So I went on to build Women Thrive - the global media platform that hosts our annual women empowerment event every March to mark and celebrate Women's History month and Women Thrive Magazine, which is our own monthly publication giving entrepreneurial women the voice to share their message and purpose with the world.

After so many life defeats, such as losing my voice and identity in my mid 20's, failing in my previous business and getting soul crushed when I was forced to give up on my mission in the past, right here right now, it all made sense. Sometimes we have to lose it all, sometimes some things will not work out and come crashing down on us so we can be redirected to our path of purpose and rebuild a new life.

As things seemed to settle in place, I finally felt at ease that I was finally travelling in the direction of my life's purpose. To my biggest surprise, this next chapter of my life I was not meant to travel alone.

Maybe the reason I had to let go of everything was because my true love was waiting for me just around the corner. It happened so suddenly that I did not see it coming, but when it did, it was the most magical and perfect moment.

I reconnected with a man I always loved and respected in my life, having known each other for more than a decade beforehand. I never imagined we could be together, as life never really brought us together in this way, but clearly this time right now we were both simply ready for love and a devoted relationship. It was magical because we already cared so much and only ever wanted the best for each other, so many years ago we set each other free. Free to be who we were, with no judgement, no restrictions, no expectations, just pure love and if we ever had the opportunity to connect we treated each other with the most love, respect and adoration for each other as individuals.

When we reconnected he looked into my eyes and asked me - "How much longer will you be running away from me? I always loved you and always will, so can we just do this now and make it forever?"

I cried because he helped me fall in love again, not with him but with myself, by accepting and loving me just as I was, which is the hardest part for all of us.

Now, a year later since we made that commitment to stop running away from each other (or running away from ourselves), we are now welcoming a new life into this world. Birthing a new soul, that will be born out of love and devotion. This is our forever love, one that does not smother, but that lets you be free just as you are.

Maybe, just maybe it was all meant to unfold just as it did and teach us all some lessons along the way. We had to go on a journey of self-discovery, healing and pain to find purpose and finally beauty in it all. I am grateful for every experience, every challenge or struggle as it made me stronger, wiser and more determined to rise and rise again.

The life crumble may come to you at the worst and least expected moments, it may shake things up, but no matter what, have faith that everything will unfold and work out in the most perfect and magical way and every bit of pain you've been through will one day make sense.

RAIMONDA JANKUNAITE

International speaker, author, visibility coach and mentor. In 2017 Raimonda founded Women in Business Club, an international community and business club for women. In just a few short years she helped thousands of women start and build successful businesses and personal brands online.

In 2020 Raimonda founded Women Thrive, with a vision to support women through the pandemic and help all women rise and thrive in business and life. Through her own life experiences of losing her voice and her confidence, Raimonda committed to building an all-inclusive media platform for women where every woman's voice and stories are celebrated. Now Women Thrive Media is a leading women's empowerment platform, hosting one of the largest annual summits online, publishing a monthly Women Thrive Magazine, Podcast and helping women share their inspiring stories in the Women Thrive book series as this.

Raimonda's mission has always been to build a supportive and inclusive platform for all women to collaborate, grow and thrive together where no woman is left behind. In her work, she not only elevates women's voices through her own media platforms but also mentors and coaches women in becoming better speakers, sought-after experts and confident thought leaders in their industry.

Join the Women Thrive global movement and be one of the brave women to share your story and change the world.

www.raimondajankunaite.com
www.womenthrivesummit.com
www.womenthrivemagazine.com

2

TRIUMPH AFTER TRAUMA

By Deepika Sandhu

I t was a normal morning in every way.

I came down the stairs of my new home, as I always do to make my coffee and transition leisurely into my day before my daughter wakes. It was just me and my daughter in this new space. Our new home was smaller than where we lived before, but it felt far more expansive, filled with all our favorite things. The beautiful deep blue velvet couch that my daughter and I picked out together. Her three foot tall, pink, stuffed unicorn Sally on the carpet next to it. My crystal collection exquisitely displayed in one corner. Our favorite paintings on the wall.

As I stood in my kitchen waiting for my coffee to brew, my eyes slowly took notice of each and every item in this space as though I was viewing it for the first time. The energy was captivating. It was putting its beautiful arms around me, lifting me up and squeezing me in the most loving embrace. Warm, happy tears filled my eyes, danced down my cheek and landed on my smiling lips.

The energy of our new space was a far cry from where I once was.

A loveless marriage.

A painful divorce.

A dismantling of everything I knew and thought I wanted.

I spent so many years trying to create a life that seemed perfect from the outside. A happy family. A beautiful house. Nice cars. Fabulous vacations. Lots of smiles posted on social media for all to see.

And now that perfectly curated life was gone.

Burnt up in an inferno of lengthy divorce proceedings, lies, arguments, trickery, pain, shame, anger, frustration and brutal sadness.

There were days when the trauma of it all was gut-wrenching.

The first few days my daughter was with her Dad at his new home was nauseatingly difficult. Away from her Mom, her normal comforts and in an entirely new space for the first time. There were nights when my daughter would refuse to sleep until she could FaceTime me so I could help her with her prayers or softly sing her to sleep. Knowing that it took her crying and screaming for her Dad to agree to call me was painful. He never told me she was upset, but I could see it in her eyes, the way only a mother can, that she was relieved through her tears to see me so I could provide her with the comfort that she needed in that moment.

Once we were off the phone, it was my turn to curl up in my bed, under my covers and just sob. It was a loud, ugly, angry cry. The one you cannot stop or control. The one where your whole body heaves. The loneliness, the sadness, the fear, the sheer madness of it all was coming out in each tear, in each sob, in each scream.

I put on a brave face everyday. A forced smile through the heartache. What choice did I have? I suppose I could have shown my then-three-year-old her mom spiraling out of control, wallowing in sadness, wondering how exactly she would go on. Instead, I choose to show her a woman finally taking a stand and moving forward, head held high. A mother who, no matter what slur was levied, what new painful words were said, what new situation we found ourselves in, would handle it with grace.

Why? Through it all, I had an intuitive nudge deep within that said, "*keep going.*"

It was my personal spiritual GPS straight from my gut showing me, moving me, guiding me towards what I *really* wanted and needed. There wasn't any rational logic associated with this sensation, no analytical reasoning that I could latch on to make it more sensical.

Trust me, I would have preferred that. As a lifelong fact-checking, checklist-making, highly logical, work hard, achieve, achieve, achieve brain, I struggled to fully embrace anything that I didn't see, touch, feel or hear for myself. If it wasn't logical, it simply wasn't something my brain could absorb.

Yet this sensation persisted. Over and over again.

Keep going.

Even when I couldn't see the way. Even when the path was completely unclear. Even when I had two choices in front of me that were both terrible and didn't know which way to go, I had this deep, overwhelming sense that a way would be shown.

Keep going.

I trusted that sense.

I didn't question it, doubt it, or vacillate from it.

Rather I surrendered to it and allowed all that was unfolding to do so. Without trying to control it. Without trying to orchestrate outcomes. Without pushing into action mode. I trusted this deep inner knowing that it was all working out as it was meant to. For someone who spent her life making things happen through hard work, grit, determination, and even sheer force, being able to let go in this way was no easy feat.

Keep going.

All of this took time. There was no magic elixir. No express pass. No secret passageway.

I had to do the work to actively, consciously let go and truly surrender to all that was happening around me, with the unwavering faith that somehow, some way it was all for my greater good. I had to let go of all the methods I employed up until this point that made me a successful business executive—a go-getter, a hard-worker, a diligent student, a confident professional. I had to release all the steps I took that gave me this seemingly perfect life—listening to my parents and their views of a good life, adhering to societal norms, and consuming television or social media. Those methods, those tools, those techniques were not the same ones that were going to yield the type of success I now needed to move forward.

Yet, even with this awareness late at night, after a full day of being brave, of putting up a good front, of trying hard to move one foot in front of the other, when I was in bed alone the trauma deep within came hurling out.

Each night through the pain, through the tears, I embraced healing techniques that allowed me to process, soothe, and love myself more deeply than I ever thought possible.

It was these healing techniques, these strategies, these beautiful support structures that made their way into my life and held me in my darkest moments when I didn't believe I had the strength to navigate all that was unraveling in front of me.

But they didn't come to me easily. They certainly did not feel natural at first. Far from it.

I read all the spiritual books I could get my hands on. Ekhart Tolle, Deepak Chopra, Oprah, Micheal Singer, Paul Coelho, Dalhi Lama, Gabrielle Bernstein, Desmond Tutu, Marianne, Wilamson. I literally read thousands and thousands of pages.

I went to temples and churches of various faiths.

I consulted astrologers, psychics and spiritualists.

I meditated on mountain tops.

I literally tried everything to get the insights I needed to transform my life. But I could never really figure out how all they were saying applied to me. Yes, I got inspired. Yes, there were amazing nuggets of wisdom that I pulled from these experiences, and which I still embrace to this day. But some of it was waaaayyyyy too woo-woo and confusing for me to practically apply and see results.

My type-A brain needed a different way. So I took woo-woo spirituality and turned it into practical spirituality for people like me.

I made it doable, tangible, a true method that could be followed. Just practical tangible steps that could be done right inside my own normal yet messy life.

Step 1 - Start Believing

It started with believing. As my marriage was unraveling, I knew I needed to rediscover myself. I needed to figure out who I was, what I wanted, and what I needed. Problem was, after almost a decade in a loveless relationship where I constantly diminished my own self worth, played small, and hid my truest desires for fear of mockery or insult, I was lost, isolated and hopeless. I had no idea where this self-discovery should even start.

Then one lazy, rainy Sunday morning while sipping coffee on my couch, I decided to look up Nicole, one of my favorite yoga teachers from when I first moved to the San Francisco Bay Area some 10 years prior. Back then, she led a Friday night restorative yoga practice that became my happy place. While my single cohorts were drinking and partying their Friday nights away, I was regularly at the yoga studio unwinding through deeply relaxing yoga poses that let me wear off the week's tension as the sun set outside the studio's floor to ceiling windows.

I hadn't attended a class with Nicole in more than seven years. But sitting on my couch that morning, I remembered that she led retreats from time to time. I Googled her name. Her new yoga studio appeared, and sure enough, she still led retreats. One of them worked perfectly for my schedule. I signed up instantly.

A few weeks later, I was reunited with Nicole at a beautiful hilltop hermitage sitting in the middle of 25 expansive acres in Northern California. The sheer beauty and simplicity of the place was breathtaking. There were rolling hills in various shades of green and brown in every direction. But more than the scenery, the energy of the place was captivating. It felt like the sun, the wind, the air, the grass, the trees were all squeezing me in the most loving embrace and saying *"you have no idea how much we are going to enjoy our time together."*

My days at the hermitage were wide open. There was a morning and evening meditation as bookends to the day, but the rest was free to sit quietly, meditate on your own, swim, hike or just soak in the silence. On most days, I found myself lying in a hammock, lost in the beautiful blue sky, the picturesque clouds, the hummingbirds, the dragonflies zipping by. It was as if the noisy exteriors of my mind were giving way to layers and layers of peace beneath them. I could simply observe without a swarm of practical, unnecessary thoughts getting in the way. It was a depth of peace that I had never experienced before.

It was in this calm and quiet that Nicole asked me a question I had never contemplated until that moment. She asked *"if you had no restrictions, no limitations and you knew you would succeed, what step would you take right now in your life? If you knew you would achieve it, what would you do?"*

The answer I got was clear: to be my most authentic self. To be the truest version of me. To stop betraying myself. To not make myself small so someone else could feel big. I needed to be me. Unapologetically, totally and completely me. I needed to leave behind all the ways I had hidden the real me to make my marriage function. I needed to not hide my interests, my hobbies, my accomplishments or my desires. I needed to not hide the real me in my own home, in daily situations, in conversations just because it was off-putting to someone else.

I liked me. I wanted to be me. All of the time. Always.

I needed to get back to my truest self. I needed to be who I was meant to be. The real me. The authentic me. The one who fully embraced all of herself rather than trying to hide herself.

Once I got this vision of what I wanted my life to be like, I started to *give* it life. I started to breathe into it. Bringing this desire to my physical world required me to treat this idea, this hope, this desire as if it already existed. I didn't simply wish that it would come true someday in the future. Instead, I believed *that it was already* true, that it was already here, that it was already my reality.

I did this by starting to feel now, in the present moment, how I would feel when all I desired showed up in my life. I started to lean into the feelings of having this life where I finally stood up as all of me, all of the time. I began to shift all of my emotions, thoughts, and beliefs into what I wanted to bring about in my life. I consciously created this by leveraging my own thoughts, feelings and energy to uplevel my own internal frequencies to align with what I wanted for myself.

I started this right there at the hermitage and I continued it daily thereafter, using simple techniques for small periods of time throughout my day. I used journaling each evening as a tool. I wrote about the life I desired as if it were already here. I used sitting in silence to feel into the energies of what I desired as my reality. Literally day-dreaming about the sensations, the feelings, the emotions that I would experience as all I wished for showed up in my life. I used mantras that I could speak out loud—in the car, in the shower, on a walk, every chance that I could find—to give my desires a voice. I placed post-it notes on my computer and on the bathroom mirror with words or feelings associated with what I wanted more of. I even used technology to set reminders on my phone to pause, reflect and feel into all I was trying to create. All of these were small yet powerful steps to consciously and intentionally not give up on myself.

I also practiced being wildly appreciative. Appreciative of this new life that I was dreaming about as well as for normal things in my everyday life that were happening now. I appreciated deeply all that had been, all that is, and all that was yet to be. Whether I liked the elements in my life or not, I believed deep in my bones that I needed to appreciate my entire journey, each step that got me to this point, no matter how painful, because it all created this awareness, this moment, this space where I could see, and feel into, a new way.

Step 2 - Start Trusting

Once I saw what I desired for myself and incorporated daily practices to believe in it, I had to learn to trust that it would all unfold for my highest good. This required letting go of self doubt. Problem was, my self-doubt was at an all-time high.

Letting myself dream and believe in a life drastically different from the one I was living was terrifying. Just the thought of leaving my marriage was scary. I was afraid of making a terrible decision.

How do I know this situation will be better? Maybe on the other side of this relationship are other bad relationships? Do I really want that? Maybe I should stay where I am? Maybe I'm being selfish? What about my daughter? What will happen to her if her family is split apart? Do I really want to do that to her?

I was gripped in fear of flipping all that was normal on its head to make some new, possibly far flung, possibly foolish, possibly really-bad-for-me idea into reality. This self-doubt was crippling. My inner saboteur created non-stop incessant chatter that spewed all of this self-doubt, negativity and catastrophized all that I was hoping to change in my life. My saboteur felt like the tightest handcuffs on my wrists, weighing me down, constraining me, paralyzing me from moving towards my change. Dismantling this was going to require big shifts. Scary shifts. But I knew that I was the one who placed these limiting beliefs, these handcuffs, on myself which meant that I was the only one who could remove them.

I decided to intentionally and consciously stop feeding my fears. I acknowledged the fear, recognized it, but actively chose to not indulge it, to not spin in it, to not let it spiral in my mind. The best way for me to do this was by humanizing my fears. I literally gave the inner critic in my head a name so that when it kicked into high gear, I could gently ask it to stop. If I wouldn't let a friend speak to me that way, I was no longer going to let myself do it either.

I named my inner saboteur Minmi. Minmi was the name of a cute little dinosaur that my daughter and I always giggled over when it popped up in her Dinosaur Encyclopedia. I spoke to Minmi.

There, there Minmi. I know you have so much to say, but right now I am going to focus on believing things will be different. I will get to your concerns another time. Literally every time my saboteur would emerge, I would say this over and over again. As I recognized this voice more, humanized it, spoke to it, it slowly started to fade to the background.

I also started filling my mind with thoughts of what could go right. I spent so much time worrying about what could go wrong. Instead of indulging that thought process, I decided to indulge the thoughts of it all working out better than I imagined. I used my daily journaling as a way to explore all that could go right when I made the changes I knew I needed to make.

I didn't fully stop my inner critic. But I did lessen its grip by giving space for that self-doubt to dissipate and replacing it with more positive views of what could be. *My daughter and I will thrive together. She will not resent her mom. This will not be her defining moment. She will grow up with a strong sense of resilience. She will never settle for less than she deserves. We will be free to explore our thoughts, our interests, our joys, together.*

This created the space, the belief, the determination to *keep going*.

Step 3 - Start Accepting and Surrendering

Even with the belief and the trust, there was one more thing I needed to do: accept and surrender to the current moment. To be at peace with what was happening, even if I didn't like it. In the height of my divorce drama, I didn't see things playing out the way they did. I had no idea that our divorce would be the most difficult, and non-amicable situation of my life.

I wanted to yell, scream, fight, argue, throw something, break something, do anything to deal with the sheer madness of it all. But I knew that fighting, yelling, lashing out wouldn't lead me to peace. Maybe I would feel like I got something off my chest. Maybe I would feel some release. But I would rather lift my gaze and stay above the fray than succumb to that. I needed to accept what was happening by not engaging in the day-to-day drama and focus instead on the outcomes I desired.

The more I trusted the eventual unfolding of all that I wanted in my life, the more my inner awareness grew. This awareness created strength, roots, a foundation that did not get swayed by the drama of my days. I no longer got jostled around by a situation, a person, a place, or an event. Not even this divorce was going to knock me off my center. It made me wobbly for sure. But as I accepted what was happening around me, I freed myself from the desire to fight, to control, to act. I lifted myself up, my energy improved, and slowly, with each step, I was creating the life I desired.

I only got to this place through practice. I practiced, practiced, practiced believing in my hopes and dreams. I practiced, practiced, practiced trusting that it would indeed all work out in my best interest, in my daughter's best interest. The more I practiced, the more rooted I became in my own beliefs.

It was not easy. Once my husband finally moved out and my daughter spent her first night away from the only home she had ever known, trying to accept and surrender to that was a herculean undertaking. It was crushing. It was devastating. I was overcome with numbness. But even in my devastated state, I accepted the moment as it was. To move forward in our lives and to live outside the confines of this marriage made her shuffling between homes an unfortunate reality. I had no choice but to live with that.

Keep going.

Step 4 - Start Allowing

Through the journey - at its best and at its worst - I always believed in the incredible, inspiring and beautiful vision of my future that was front and center in my mind's eye, in my heart, in my innermost self. I nurtured the belief that this future would unfold for me. I trusted in it. I could see it magically forming each and every day, little by little.

Even in my hardest moments, even when the pain of my reality was piercing, I never lost sight of what I was creating, where I was heading, and how it would feel when I was there. I relied on my simple daily practices—journaling, believing, sitting in silence, trusting—to guide me each and every day to stay in the energies of it all unfolding for our highest good. I kept feeding the vision, fueling the feelings, loving into all that I was creating. I didn't get in its way. I didn't try to control the events or the outcomes. I stayed open to how it all would happen. I kept my gaze high, above the drama, always focused instead on the eventual outcome that I knew in my bones would be mine.

Firmly standing on the other side of my own struggles, I can say this existence, this new reality, this life is all that I envisioned for myself and more. I stepped into the real me. I became who I was meant to become. I landed in this exact spot that is *beyond* the vision I had for myself. It is all I desired and more.

The tears were still streaming down my face when my daughter came down the stairs. She snuck up gently behind me as I was lost, gazing at our new home, feeling its powerful and loving energy, reliving bits and pieces of the past and all it took to get us to this moment today. A today where my daughter enjoys two loving homes, with two happy parents comfortable in their own existence. A today where there is no more tension, stress or fear filling the rooms of our home. A today where she is fully free to be all of who she is becoming, and so am I. A today that is filled with so much laughter, fun and beautiful simple everyday moments. A today where I no longer have to play small or diminish my worth, and can truly show up courageously and confidently as all of me. A today that allows us to dream bigger, to desire even more, and to believe new ways are always possible. A today that is filled with the strength of knowing that hard times yield magical ones. A today filled with love.

She took my hand in hers and gave three soft squeezes. It was our secret code. A silent way of saying *I love you* whenever we were out and about together. I looked down at her smiling, happy face. I squeezed her hand four times. Secret code for *I love you too.*

DEEPIKA SANDHU

ABOUT THE AUTHOR

Deepika is a Silicon Valley Business Executive, Authenticity Coach, and author of *Hello Universe, It's Me*. Deepika's mission is to inspire busy, hard working professionals to go from overwhelmed, demotivated, burnt out and exhausted, to living a life that is authentic and true to you in every possible way. In Deepika's talks, 1:1 coaching and courses, she shares her signature approach to help you create massive breakthroughs in your normal, everyday life and leave the burnout behind once and for all.

www.deepikasandhu.co

3

THE MESSY MADNESS THAT SET ME FREE

By Vicky Midwood

T *his is it.*
     I'm Fu*ked.

My biggest fear was now my reality, I had finally lost the plot, I thought I was a 'basket case,' that I'd finally gone mad, and it was all my fault.

The grandiose idea I'd clung onto for over two decades that somehow I was special and different, I was invincible, that MY body and brain would carry on no matter what abuse I threw at them year after year, was smashed to smithereens.

I was seeing and hearing things, wandering the local Highstreet, with my 6 year old daughter in tow.

Talking to myself, and to people who didn't exist.

Trying to break into cars that I thought were mine.

You'd think after the ambulance was called and I ended up in a hospital bed, things would be sorted.

Think again.

I was kept for a few hours and then sent home!

NO recollection of how I got home.

Did I walk the 3.5 miles home? Get a cab?

I'll never know.

I just know that I did get home, and I was still seeing and hearing things that weren't there.

I was now convinced I was definitely crazy.

Yet here's the truly CRAZY thing...

I had totally lost the need to have a drink!

Poof, just like that, my desire for alcohol had been totally removed. Wow!

But was this madness the price I now had to pay to be sober? Was this my penance, my punishment for all the upset and chaos I had caused over the last 22 years?

Fast forward 2 days, and I'm in Rehab.

It was thanks to my GP who spotted I was in severe alcohol withdrawal immediately and made a phone call. I was whisked away to the nearest Priory Rehab Hospital and put in a private room.

I was monitored every 20 mins.

For 48 hours it was touch and go as to whether or not my heart and brain would be able to keep me alive!

No Such Thing as Coincidence

Let's just dive into the 'power of the universe' and being careful what you wish for a moment, and why I just STOPPED drinking.

As a functioning alcoholic, I'd NEVER had even ONE alcohol-free day in over 16 years.

Which made just stopping drinking completely a pretty stupid and dangerous thing to do, right?

Wishes do come true.

See, years before, I was struggling with teenage bulimia and wanting to end it all. It was just too hard and exhausting to keep doing what I was doing. Stealing food, bingeing, throwing up in secret multiple times a day, addicted to exercise and laxatives.

I wished I was an alcoholic (WTF!).

I know, I know, that seems madness, but with food addiction, you can't just stop eating and never eat again.

My thinking was, if I was an alcoholic, I could just stop drinking and never have to drink again and I would be 'cured.'

Well, I got what I wished for!

But I hadn't been clear in my request. I wanted to swap bulimia for alcohol, but instead I got it added. Now I was doubly addicted, with one fueling the other!

And that was my existence from age 18-35 until the trajectory of my life was changed forever...

With a last-minute change of plan on a road trip that meant I physically wasn't able to get my hands on an alcoholic drink for just over 4 hours. By that time, withdrawal was kicking in.

That gives you a clue as to how great my body and brain's tolerance and reliance on wine and beer was just to function 'normally.'

I believe those circumstances were no 'coincidence' but were orchestrated by a power greater than me, stepping in to help me to do what I couldn't for myself.

This power helped me to put down the booze once and for all and get my life on track.

It helped me to step into my purpose to help free others from addictions.

Gratitude is a big part of my B.L.A.S.T. Method to Feeling Fabulously Free.

The B.L.A.S.T. method empowers strong but struggling high achievers, people pleaser perfectionists (like me) put down food, alcohol, or both, and let go of the feelings of guilt and shame around feeling out of control and 'not good enough.'

Becoming Sane & Sober!

Rehab both here in the UK and South Africa was an experience I am so grateful for.

I had the space and time to learn about me.

Who was Vicky, before this opportunity? I genuinely did not know!

I got to understand my brain, the power words, of childhood trauma. There had been plenty of that with a perfectionist workaholic Dad who didn't believe in mental illness and a Mum with bi-polar disorder.

I am so grateful I was able to gain awareness of the unconscious programming from my early years and start the conscious re-programming that enabled me to lay down the foundations for creating the person I am today before I left.

What I learned was that you have to know and accept who you are BEING now in order to take responsibility for BECOMING the person you want to be. This is just one of the B's we cover in my B.L.A.S.T. method and VIP Fast Track to Freedom Days.

What happens in rehab is something people are fascinated by. Is it like what you see on TV and in films? The answer is: pretty much, yeah!

Group therapy where everyone sits in a circle to share their experiences, feelings and thoughts, and listen to others do the same, plus attendance at an ANONYMOUS meeting every single day for the duration of the stay.

Re-Defining Me

Standing up and saying "My name is Vicky and I'm an alcoholic" quite frankly really pissed me off. I was not, and I am not a label or a behaviour (neither is anyone!)

I hate labels; they make me feel uncomfortable and cross. It goes back to my Mum being referred to as 'a Manic Depressive' in my early teens and me thinking, "no, that's not who she is, she's my Mum, with an illness that I hate!"

In fact, I loathe the word 'alcoholic' so much that I will not use it except to talk about my story. The term alcohol-dependent sits better with me. Words, names and labels are powerful, as are the associations, interpretations and perceptions we attach to them.

B.L.A.S.T Heals with Words

Language—words and how we understand and use them—is one of the L's in the B.L.A.S.T. method to freedom from addiction, guilt, pain and shame. It plays a huge part in transforming feelings of self-loathing to self-loving, as does *letting go of labels.*

Feelings

Those first two weeks in rehab were eye-opening, upsetting and frustrating.

I was completely detached from my feelings; I had to be given a handout with pictures of emoji's to try to connect to my emotions. I wore so many masks, I had no clue who I really was.

This is when I understood that I had always felt like I needed to please others to feel 'worthy', or 'good enough.' I was completely disconnected from who I was or what I felt. To say I was 'lost' is the only way I can explain it.

Allowing re-connection with B.L.A.S.T.

I now understood what Gabor Maté meant when he stated that "the opposite of Addiction is Connection." I was disconnected not only from myself, but other people.

I realised I had no friends. That began when I shunned a typical teenage social life for a love affair with stuffing my face with cake and ice-cream, then sticking my head down the loo every weekend.

I flunked my 'A' levels, got work in a bar, and found addict husband #1 (sex & gambling), aged 18. Once I was married and qualified as a fitness instructor and personal trainer at age 21, my life revolved around working and feeding my food and alcohol addiction.

Divorced and drinking even more, I found addict husband #2 (alcohol & work), a chef and restaurateur. I ended up running the bar-side of his business as well as my own fitness business.

Divorced again, and bankrupt with a 3-year-old by the time I moved to London to be with potential husband #3, I was even more alone and disconnected. My drinking escalated significantly.

Rehab started me on the path to reconnecting with myself and others for the first time in over two decades.

I learned about the brain, about what addiction really was. I realised I loved learning. I decided to go back to education once I returned home. The seeds for learning had been sown. I haven't stopped learning since!

I felt driven and inspired to help change the lives of millions. Millions globally who have succumbed, like me, to the social conditioning, stereotyping, labelling people as an illness or a diagnosis. Dismantling the false (BS) beliefs about addictions just being a mental health issue (they're not!).

After 3 months in rehab, I arrived back home.

Real Life

I came home and tried to re-integrate into 'normal life.' All I can say is: it was bloody hard!

I still was trying to discover WHO I was and how to BE me.

Rehab hadn't given me all the tools I needed. Don't get me wrong, it was a great start, but the real rehab begins when you leave rehab!

I'd not worked for 6 weeks before the universe stepped in and did a 'one eighty' with my life. Now I had to think about how I was going to earn a living and just what I was able to do, work-wise. I had to get help with rent and living costs.

I was embarrassed and ashamed to be living on government handouts and was now determined to change that.

I also needed to extricate the male person (not potential husband #3, he was long gone) still in my life who was a big factor in my drinking going to a whole new level yet again.

Looking back all these years later, I genuinely don't know how I did it.

I was building my health & fitness business, teaching exercise classes and personal training most weekend mornings. Studying for my teaching degree. Learning CBT (Cognitive Behavioural Therapy), NLP (Neuro-Linguistic Programming), and Addiction Psychology, and doing a work placement in a college of further education. All of this while trying to run my home and be a good Mum to my now 7 year old daughter and attend regular AA meetings.

I was under more stress in those first five to seven years after rehab than I think I had ever been before in my life. I wasn't blotting it out anymore with booze. I had to face it head-on.

What I didn't appreciate then was the effect it was having on me physiologically as well as psychologically. As the sole income earner, I always felt the pressure.

I can tell you getting off the benefits system in the UK completely is an absolute nightmare!

My old exercise addiction thoughts were creeping back in. I found myself feeling more and more out of control around chocolate and coffee. I rarely ate a proper meal, telling myself I didn't have the time to sit down and eat. Sound familiar? Worryingly, I found my mind drifting frequently back to my weight and appearance and even to throwing up...

WTF!

What the actual fuck?

Was I really going to allow myself to go backwards?

To go back down into THAT rabbit hole again.

No! I was not.

I wanted answers: what was I missing? I knew by now that addiction is not just a mental illness, or a personality type, so I chose to take my knowledge of nutrition, physiology, biochemistry, and neuropsychology to a new level.

Bacteria, parasites, dysbiosis, the gut-**biome** and the link between the **gut-brain** connection were not that familiar to me then (they are very familiar now), but I knew on an intuitive level this would be where my studies and search for answers should be headed.

These are some of the B's in my B.L.A.S.T method to feeling fabulously free.

I studied the importance of basic lifestyle factors like **blood sugar management**, sleep, stress management and **Boundaries** (two more B's!) and the environment you are living and working in.

I'd love to tell you I sorted myself out and felt better. But the truth is, I didn't.

I got worse, and I wanted answers.

I was exhausted and struggling, but no one knew it. On the outside, I was always full of energy and fun, but it was all an act.

In the mornings, I didn't want to get out of bed and face the day. Some days, those old familiar suicidal thoughts came flooding in like a tsunami. I was terrified I was suffering with depression, but there was also a niggling feeling that there was something wrong physically.

I was aching, permanently, especially in my back. My body temperature was going haywire. I felt my limbs were heavy. My energy was tanked and I was struggling to maintain my weight.

I struggled like this for nearly 3 years, just putting on a brave face and crying inside. Perhaps you can relate? Outwardly it appears you have everything together while inwardly you are falling apart.

My GP was no help whatsoever, first telling me it could be a virus. Next it was early menopause. On the third visit I was offered antidepressants!

I left without that prescription, shaking my head in resigned disbelief that pills were being offered as the 'solution.' I'd seen those things destroy my mother's quality of life for over 40 years and trigger my Dad to commit suicide.

Enough is Enough!

I decided to contact a health coach I'd followed for years and get a full comprehensive blood test done. Once I had my consultation with him on the results, I had many of my answers. Hashimoto's thyroiditis (an autoimmune disease affecting the thyroid gland).

Heading for a heart attack and diabetes.

My health was a mess, but he told me exactly what I needed to do to heal and feel better fast, without taking conventional medication.

This is when I grasped the importance of the 'T' in my B.L.A.S.T. method - **taking** the appropriate action at the right **time** and **talking to experts.**

Healing The Gut

Reducing inflammation had to be the first step, then healing the gut. I had basically annihilated my gut lining through years of starvation, binge eating, vomiting, laxative abuse and drinking vast amounts of wine and beer daily.

I was unknowingly exacerbating the damage with inflammatory food on the go; too much caffeine, stress, cardio and intense physical training. Not enough yoga, stretching and relaxation.

This is why education is a key part of how I help people to heal and re-connect back to themselves and their body.

The body gives us signs: bloating, gas, pain, constipation or diarrhea. But we are taught to ignore them, with the thought "it'll go away." Or we try to 'fix' them with over-the-counter medications. In the case of disordered eating, we simply ignore the signs completely or punish our body with excess exercise or restrictions.

Embracing Change With Curiosity

I did make massive changes. Changing my exercise routine, taking good quality supplements to heal my gut and support my liver.

Reprogramming the beliefs and language I had fired and wired around weight and size.

I made those changes fun, simple, doable and straightforward by *giving myself permission to get curious,* and not feel pressured to do things a specific way.

'Keep it simple' is something I stand by in everything I do in my business and my own life. Giving myself and my clients permission to just get curious and have a go has been a game-changer to their outcomes and to mine.

The cravings for chocolate went, my aches disappeared, my weight started to decrease, my sleep improved, and I felt re-energised.

The Heart Of Stress and Healing

Unfortunately, I did have that heart attack as predicted, but it wasn't a surprise. Heart attacks are on both sides of my family, and it was triggered by a cascade of stressful events in late 2017. This is why eliminating stress and improving sleep are the two key 'S's' in the B.L.A.S.T Method along with saying "NO" to others in order to say "YES" to yourself.

Thanks to my knowledge and background in exercise and fitness, physically I knew how to recover. I was conventional medication free within 3 months

I believe we get to learn from everything, and this was yet another opportunity for me to experience first-hand, the very real roller coaster of emotions that go with the sudden realisation that "you could have died, but you didn't."

I knew how lucky I was not to have become a statistic.

Fortunately, I now know the human body and brain are amazing, and designed to heal. All we need to do is tune in to what they are telling us and do what is asked.

Adversity to Advantage

Turning **adversity to advantage along with an attitude of gratitude** is something I teach and highly recommend. These 'A's are a part of the B.L.A.S.T. method along with allowing. Allowing yourself to feel your feelings, but reminding yourself that feelings or 'emotions' are just energy in motion. If we acknowledge them, then let them go and flow rather than hanging on to them, we get to feel more joy and freedom than we ever thought possible.

I surrounded myself with health 'geeks' and like-minded integrative, functional and holistic wellbeing experts over the years. Continuously educating myself and working to bring together all the elements of the B.L.A.S.T. Method.

Based in science, psychology, neurology, biochemistry, personal experience and *the three key principles of change (A.R.T.) - Awareness, Responsibility, Taking Action,* I have created a simple solution to eliminating addictions and living a life that you love.

BE-ing Open to Opportunities

Over time, along my incredible journey I have come to understand that compassion, curiosity and courage are needed to embrace all that life has to offer. I know that I will never have to face more than I can handle, even if that includes broken bones, bankruptcy and physical violence. I also know that asking for help is a sign of great strength and growth mindset, not of weakness or lack.

I have learned and experienced some amazing things though being open to what's out there and what's possible. This has included meditating with monks in Thailand and taking plant medicine with a female shaman in Colombia. During these experiences, I received the spiritual download that *whole person healing and education are my true purpose.*

Lockdown during the pandemic allowed me yet another life changing opportunity.

The chance to slow the fu*k down.

It meant I had time to get really clear and focused on my business, to really define and align how best to serve the hundreds of educated, smart, outwardly successful middle aged women and men struggling.

To serve people who are mentally and physically fighting with food, weight, body image, gut issues, alcohol dependence and anxiety.

Assisting those living with the guilt and shame that accompanies the lies and manipulation required to hide what's really going on and pretending everything is 'fine'

Experience has taught me that **Retreats** and **VIP Days** are by far the most effective and time efficient way to do just that.

The B.L.A.S.T method has all the elements needed to heal body, mind and soul by eliminating addictions, bogus beliefs, lousy language and stinking thinking.

One full *FEEL FABULOUS VIP DAY* with me can exceed the benefits of our having 8 weeks of one-to-one weekly sessions.

Having the space and time to fully focus on you, whether it is a VIP day or a longer retreat without distractions or interruptions, is the best way for you to reconnect and get to know yourself again. We can create a personal plan that allows you to step into being the person you really want to be: compulsion, obsession and addiction free. *Living rather than existing. Thriving, not just surviving.*

My messy madness back in 2005 has allowed me to *FEEL FABULOUS* in my own skin and BE free to be me.

I'm no different to you. I wasn't broken. I wasn't bad.

I wasn't flawed, and neither are you.

If you have the clarity, courage, curiosity, commitment, and burning desire to create a new version of you, and you are ready to invest in yourself, your health, and a happy, fulfilling future: I'd love to have a chat with you.

VICKY MIDWOOD

ABOUT THE AUTHOR

Vicky Midwood, AKA The Addictions Eliminator, is an integrative health, nutrition, and lifestyle coach who has been in the fitness and wellness world for over 30 years

Creator of the BLAST Method to Feeling Fabulously Free, based on science and personal experience, she helps smart, educated, high achievers over 35 reduce anxiety, shame and guilt by eliminating the compulsion to self-sabotage with food or alcohol or both.

She works with women and men in-person via 3, 5 & 7 Day Small Group Retreats, VIP Days and online through weekly one-to-one sessions over 3-6 months.

www.vickymidwood.com

4

HOW EMBRACING MY ROOTS FUELED MY PASSION INTO PURPOSE

By Neetu Deol Jhaj

T he same vivid conversation played in my mind countless times before I drove myself to my maternal grandmother's home for the first time at 16 years old.

I walked in and sat down in a familiar space – her living room with a sewing machine situated between her basket of yarn and dining table. As long as I could remember, I would come to *Biji's* home and watch her knit her exquisite sweaters for hours and hours on end. I was always fascinated by the soft wool texture and the way each sweater would come together, sleeve by sleeve, neckline to hem.

Unbeknownst to me, these sweaters would kickstart an important trajectory in my life. On a past visit, Biji shared that the sweaters she had been knitting had been sold at Nordstroms. While Biji's sweaters made it into a store with an impressive caliber, the woman whom she found via a newspaper ad to help her reaped the majority of the profits, taking advantage of a middle-aged immigrant woman whose circumstances to survive in a country foreign to her upbringing did not afford her the possibility to own and defend her intellectual property.

Not understanding the magnitude of a store she had never had the opportunity to set foot in, but understanding how important deadlines and reputation were, Biji worked tirelessly to knit her high-in-demand sweaters until her fingers could no longer keep up. She gave knitting everything she had because this skill is what helped provide for her family when she immigrated to the United States, and what provided the opportunity for her son to start his journey at engineering school.

Looking down at her frail fingers and up at her tired eyes on that day, I told Biji the future would be different. I was going to make up for the moments of pride she lost whilst in survival mode on new soil. Biji's motivation to start work and life anew in a new country inspired me. Having developed a keen interest in the art of designing clothing myself, I told Biji I wanted to fuel this family passion and skilled art form into something meaningful. I did not know yet where life would lead me, but I knew I wanted to create and lead a life of impact and make her sacrifices worthwhile. Had it not been for her life decisions and desire to move the needle forward for the next generation, I would not have had the opportunity for life itself.

Above all, one thing was definite – my family lineage grounds my existence and within it, are embedded rock-solid roots of resiliency and hard work; there was no way something remarkable could not be made of Biji's fate.

Biji was surprised when I told her I wanted to enhance the course of life for her. She smiled and told me in Punjabi, "I don't expect anything. As parents and grandparents, we work hard so our kids and grandchildren have a better opportunity to succeed and have a better life than we did. I just want you to focus on educating yourself. Whatever you do in life and whatever job you have, always educate yourself at every step. Someone may have taken my skill from me, but they can never take your education from you."

Rarely has a word resonated as strongly for me as that of *resilience* — the one that brought generations of our family members here, all with a common permeating thread: to work hard and give their children a chance at education and opportunity.

At 16, I felt remorse for not giving my parents and grandparents enough credit earlier for the resident alien card they had to carry daily until they became U.S. citizens. It was not until I took time to understand that the struggle for immigrants was unfathomably real, and the sacrifices they made to open the door to the world I was enjoying did not come without a multitude of hardships. When children of immigrants do come to this realization, there is widespread desire to pay it forward and do even greater good than the prior generation, to do something exceptional and most importantly, to do something with impact.

I didn't know at the age of 16 what that impact would be and where life would lead me, but I knew I wanted to contribute in a positive way for the generations that would follow. If I did not make a change going forward, what happened to my grandmother could become repeated history.

Getting Acquainted With Leadership

For me, this started with leadership.

I was fortunate to shadow a mother who completely immersed herself in our cultural art forms, from dancing to theatre, taking a lead to help direct theatrical performances and dance forms like giddha.

Following in her footsteps, I joined various service-centered organizations in high school, while completely relishing in my passions of designing Indian lenghas and choreographing cultural dances, the combination of which helped me feel harmonized with my heritage. My mom was instrumental in helping me bring to life, through boutiques in India, hand-drawn sketches of Indian clothing I would design.

I learned early on that those in positions of leadership tend to get greater opportunities and respect. My mom was my best example of a woman who made it in corporate America despite the odds stacked against her; regardless of cultural, linguistic and financial barriers early on, she persevered by ascending through the leadership ranks.

My mom told me to get back up and try again every time I was defeated in my quest to serve in a leadership role in grade school. I was taught to never back down from anything we feel even remotely being capable of achieving.

Despite earlier defeats, leadership was not an end-all for me. In high school, I became President of the Indian Student Association and served as Editor-in-Chief of my school yearbook my senior year. At every milestone when I would share the news with Biji, she would share my excitement; the support she and my mother provided me was a welcome change and meant the world.

For a young, brown, Indian girl growing up in a traditional and strict household with two paternal grandparents who showcased a strong preference for boys over girls, visits with Biji were refreshing and provided me with an optimism about a girl's place in the world. I was delighted when Biji and my mom's brother convinced my mom to let me go away to college despite reservations in the home about a girl leaving the household before marriage. They felt it was important for me to become independent, start to understand the real world out of the shadow of a highly protective household, and most importantly, to discover myself. That encouragement and confidence further fueled my drive to open the door one day to educational opportunity, not only for the preceding generation, but the one that would follow.

In college, I found great joy in being awarded as part of the winning team that took home the trophy for most funds raised for St. Jude's Children's Research Hospital. With the encouragement of my peers, I served as part of the President's cabinet and oversaw all school programming for students in an appointed role, before I was elected as a Senator and then Senate Pro Temp of our 19,000 student body population.

At each facet of my leadership experience, my mother and Biji reminded me that if I worked hard and kept focus and a humble outlook, that I could truly achieve any goal or idea I put out into the world. The key piece of advice I was reminded of was that even if I did not reach an aim I wanted to achieve, what I gained in the process was invaluable information and lessons that would be vital to future success. For me, the process of evolving as a leader was the confidence it was instilling in me, the grit to withstand criticism and the ability to resolve injustices head on. These experiences were shaping me as a young brown girl who was trying to figure out where she stood in the world.

These experiences were also igniting an energy to fuel my family's efforts into something meaningful so their hard work would not be in vain. I did not simply want to ride the coattails of those who came before me; instead, it was important to pay it forward. I became a CASA (Court Appointed Special Advocate) for foster children in my volunteer time while I figured out what part of the start-up world I had an interest in, I would eventually become part of.

The Start-Up World

My mom got me my first experience in the start-up world at the age of 18, which helped me brush up on my communication and gain greater confidence in working as part of a team. Not satisfied with the scripts I was provided to make cold calls as a member of the joint sales and marketing team, I developed a version I felt comfortable using. On one particular day, I was pulled into the office by the CFO. I thought surely I must be presenting something wrong to potential customers. Instead, I was congratulated because my cold calls and script had been successful; movie production conglomerate Metro-Goldwyn-Mayer (MGM) was now a customer; the nice bonus on my paycheck actually made it believable. I was also told my script would be utilized going forward. While I maintained my cool in the CFO's office, inside I was doing cartwheels. This small victory and work experience gave me greater confidence in my abilities. I thought about Biji and how I wanted her to experience this same feeling of value and recognition for her craft.

Much the same as my mother did for me, I thought about my future children and knew I wanted to get them involved in work they found interesting or exciting, to help develop them as people, give them an opportunity to explore their interests, and overall, to gain valuable life experience.

The company I worked for at the age of 18 was acquired a few years later by a Fortune 100 company. My mother then became a partner in a new software company. Initially as part of management in the marketing team, and then as head of public relations, I gained extensive experience in a number of areas ranging from customer service, to governance, compliance and scaling a company. It has been exciting to apply this experience to our current businesses.

Shortly after marriage, my husband and his family asked me to join the family business, a unique concept with quick service restaurants inclusive of Subway, Taco Bell and Pizza Hut housed within Shell-branded convenience markets. For over two decades, Countryside has been a franchisee and licensee of national brands. Today, Countryside has evolved into a corporation that provides over five hundred jobs across its quick-service restaurant, construction, and retail development arms with an expanded business portfolio which includes Countryside retail centers and Countryside Car Washes. Countryside is a byproduct of decades of hard work by my husband's father and our family to achieve the American dream. This dream is a realization that you can come from nothing and create the foundation for an empire that can set up generations of family members from children to grandchildren I was excited to join the family business in large part because our families had similar immigrant backgrounds and shared experiences in their early days in America as farmworkers. To be a part of a collaborative effort to expand the business footprint and family legacy, has been both gratifying and inspiring. Collectively, we have gained extensive business acumen and knowledge in operating successful businesses; working together with my husband and family has cemented a path of success we can pass on to the next generation.

The Evolution of Rehna Raiya

The culmination of experience across various spectrums of management and operation of the family business led to the foundation of Rehna Raiya, a retail clothing brand that naturally evolved to fill gaps I observed in girls' clothing. Rehna and Raiya are my daughters' names and the line serves as an empowering and uplifting clothing brand for girls and women. I observed in my own children how clothing could make a girl feel empowered or very easily disempowered. It was important for me to ensure their experience was always positive and memorable.

When I saw the struggle girls faced with wearing one-piece jumpsuits, I created and launched the industry's first-to-market one-piece jumpsuit that can be unsnapped to a two-piece jumpsuit; our patent-pending jumpsuits allow girls to independently use the restroom with ease. Raiya was drawn to help find a resolution to another challenge in the girls' clothing industry: finding matching shorts to go with every dress so girls can participate in any activity without being limited by what *they choose* to wear. With no place to find this exact match, we decided to make matching shorts with every dress in all our collections, from girls to women.

With the addition of empowerment tees in our collection with words like "UNSTOPPABLE" and "Future," our primary goal is to help remind girls of their worth and importance. We designed our packaging and clothing tags with a simple slogan that when wholeheartedly embraced, can have life-changing effects on young impressionable girls:

I love myself.

I believe in myself.

I am UNSTOPPABLE!

While the aforementioned is the more practical segment of the brand, the sentimental piece is of significant mention. Rehna Raiya was launched on August 4th, the day of Biji's 82nd birthday. I called Biji to surprise her with the news; up until this moment, Biji did not have the slightest clue that I had been working on this launch for over two years. I told Biji she would no longer be defined as an immigrant woman whose circumstances rendered her unable to receive recognition for her talents. Her family lineage would now sit at the helm of a clothing company named after her great-granddaughters, that would donate a portion of all proceeds to educate young girls.

Joy and shock do not begin to describe the emotions elicited by Biji, especially when she heard we want to use this line to empower young girls and educate them; choked up and barely able to say a few words, she was beaming with pride over the phone. The pandemic did not allow me to share the news in person with Biji, but through her voice and appreciation, I knew what I was embarking on was going to make the last few years of Biji's life both rejuvenating and rewarding. A euphoric feeling filled my soul that day; the deep roots of my family grew an extension and enveloped me in an encouraging embrace. I had turned a passion into purpose and the journey now began to make that impact.

Never Dream Without Action

The eventual launch of Rehna Raiya was truly a therapeutic moment for me. For two years before launch, I had this constant conflict between whether I should or should not launch the line. A list of "what if's" prevented me from moving forward.

When I stopped to reflect on the responsibility I had to my daughters, and the path they would follow in the shadow of my footsteps, I charted my eventual step forward.

I realized my fear of not starting the line was greater than the fear of starting it. I never wanted my daughters to question, "Mom, why didn't you do it?" Afraid of any limitations they might place on themselves if I did not show them a strong and courageous example, I gathered the strength from my grandmother's story and I knew I had to show my own daughters that not only a woman can, but *SHE DID*.

Above all, I decided I could no longer serve myself and my children adequately and nurture them as I desired to, if I simply sat there imagining and thinking about unfulfilled dreams and doing nothing to manifest them into a reality they could see and experience for themselves. *Deep down inside, I knew I never wanted to be the person who just sat and wondered, who dreamed without action.*

F.A.I.L.

At the end of the day, I asked myself, what's the worst that could happen? That big word F.A.I.L. might descend upon me? When I truly sat down to reflect on the intricacies of the word, I looked up FAIL on the internet and gained such great insight. F.A.I.L. is First Attempt In Learning. I read those powerful words again and again on the screen.

At the crux of it, isn't that what we are on this earth to do? To learn, educate ourselves and apply what we have learned to better life in some way for ourselves, for our families, and for others?

Further, I knew I could never fail my daughters as there were valuable lessons, valuable time we would spend together and a confidence they would gain in being a part of something that would make life better for other girls who would be empowered and educated in the process. Knowing I would be contributing in such a positive way to the self-confidence of my own daughters and others' daughters we could positively impact, outweighed any perceived failure I may encounter starting this line. *If we as women look back at the young and influential age of five years to sixteen years of age, imagine where the progress of women would already be had we had the chance to be empowered at that young an age.* Imagine learning to push past any limitations posed at a young age rather than learning in adulthood when most women first embark on those baby steps to become empowered.

Above all, how could I FAIL when I had an entire village that came before me who helped set up the foundation my children now have at their disposal? I am so grateful I never had to start from the bottom, working in the fields and on the assembly line of factories, as my parents and in-laws did when they immigrated to the United States.

Just as we hoist our children up and place them on our shoulders when they can't see the path someone has already traveled, there is an entire village who has done that for me, and for those efforts that came before mine, I am eternally grateful.

The Power of NO

This exercise of dissecting the word F.A.I.L. reminded me of the same feeling I had eight years ago when I teeter-tottered whether I should take initiative to institute cultural change at a country club where predominantly men served on the board of directors. Observing a lack of representation of the women's voice on the board, I wanted the baby girl I was pregnant with to grow up in a social organization of inclusion. On my first inquiry to the then COO of the organization about a position on the membership vetting committee, I was told there was no availability. On my second inquiry, he looked right at my ever-growing belly of 7.5 months pregnant and said, "Nothing right now. But I will let you know if something ever comes up." I knew that meant no.

With not a single minority on this historically male board, I could not ignore how that lack of representation made me feel. I got in touch with a friend who had a direct connection to the sitting president of the board, and I presented one question. For an otherwise qualified person, did the fact that I was a brown woman or a pregnant woman or both factor into the "no" I received? Within a few days, I received formal notice that a position had opened up for me on the membership committee.

To cut a long story short, I did my time on the membership committee, learning the intricacies and makeup of the board and its foundation until I myself was elected to the board a few years later. In my third year on the board, I was elected to serve as the first female President in the 30-year history of the board. I did not take my position on this historically male board lightly and strived to open up the door for other women. While I faced many challenges posed by a couple of male board members who struggled with taking direction from a woman and someone almost half their age, the uphill climb was worth it when a woman whose application to the board was previously denied, now serves on the board.

What did I learn? The power of "no" is actually very effective, making us work harder to persist until we prevail. Yes *can* exist *if* we are willing to commit ourselves enough to get that yes. As women, we undoubtedly have to go the extra step to create a seat at the table; it is a rarity if anyone pulls up a chair for us to sit down. Rather than sulk at the disadvantage women undoubtedly face, turning the power of "no" into yes actually makes us feel really proud of how far women have come and fuels an indescribable satisfaction of continuing to new heights and overcoming barriers for women as a whole.

Embracing My Roots

The connection I have to my roots is what continues to propel me forward in every endeavor of my life. I might not have given enough respect nor shown enough gratitude for my immigrant roots as a young girl, but I can never again forget where I come from – the culmination of the above-mentioned events is what has brought me to this day. The day I started to embrace my roots was life-changing: it kick-started my evolution to the person I am today; the opportunities I have, and the valuable lessons I learned in life and leadership put me on a path for success.

From my mother and Biji, I learned the grit and hard work to start something anew, how to fuel my passion into purpose, and to keep moving forward in the face of adversity.

From working alongside my father-in-law, husband and Countryside family, I have gained extensive business acumen, how to bridge community relationships in our hometown, and an in-depth understanding of businesses across sectors inclusive of gas stations and quick-service restaurants.

From countless women who have served as inspiration or as

mentors, I have learned to embrace myself for exactly what and who I am.

My culture and roots have taught me that persistence and working hard for a seat at the table is a very real challenge, but one that is attainable and fulfilling beyond measure.

The Look Forward

With tremendous work still yet to be done, it comes time to work continually to lay the foundation for youth following in our footsteps.

My hope is that every young girl is inspired to be remembered as someone who made whatever impact she could, with whatever ability and passion that fueled her, in this contribution to the advancement of girls. I want every girl to step up her worth in her own eyes and know she has the opportunity Biji never had: to stand up for herself in the face of adversity.

Above all, my hope is for every girl and woman to embrace herself just as she is, with the roots that define her, and learn to propel herself to the future she desires for herself.

NEETU DEOL JHAJ

ABOUT THE AUTHOR

A native of the Silicon Valley, Neetu began her corporate career in the start-up industry before she had her daughters Rehna and Raiya, her greatest accomplishment.

Today, along with her family, Neetu is a co-owner of Countryside Corporation, a construction and retail development company that owns and operates multi-national brands inclusive of Shell, Subway and Taco Bell.

As the Founder of empowerment clothing line Rehna Raiya, Neetu strives to pay it forward to the next generation of girls. Through the development of patent-pending industry concepts to resolve gaps in girl's clothing and up-lifting messaging, the empowerment and advancement of young girls is Neetu's motivation to make a positive imprint every day. Close to her heart is her service on various education-centered non-profits to help youth create the future they see for themselves. When she is not working, Neetu loves to enjoy various outdoor activities with her family, inclusive of pickleball.

www.rehnaraiya.com email: admin@rehnaraiya.com

5

LIGHT THROUGH THE DARKNESS

MY JOURNEY THROUGH TRAUMA AND DISEASE

By Angelic Ingram

We met on a blind date.

I had sworn I would never go on another one after a disastrous blind date my sister set me up on with her friend's son many years prior. I thought, if my own sister didn't have a clue, then who would?

So when my friend called me one day to invite me to go dancing with her and her boyfriend (and her boyfriend's roommate, whom I had never met), I gracefully declined the offer. Then she called back, apparently having no luck with the rest of her single friends list, to try and persuade me to join them. After going back and forth with her on the phone, and my own roommate commenting, "Just go and have fun, it's not like you have to marry the guy!" I finally decided to go and just enjoy a night out dancing.

I was just about to turn 30, and I was smitten with his charm, dazzling smile and confidence from the moment we met. He was tall, with short dark hair and warm brown eyes, and very handsome (picture Ben Affleck!). He was a true gentleman and we connected immediately.

As we got to know each other in the following weeks, we fell madly in love, and our relationship moved fast. So fast, in fact, that we decided to tie the knot on our one-year anniversary of dating in February 2000, and we couldn't wait, we wanted to get married in two weeks! We just felt right about it and so we went with our hearts.

Things took what seemed like an immediate wrong turn from the moment we said "I do"—but it's not what you might think. It had nothing to do with my loving new husband, and everything to do with my new in-laws.

Never did I imagine that my life would take the turn it did. I suppose no one ever thinks that they would face trauma or adversity in their life for that matter. It just happens, and it can impact your life forever.

The Dark

I used to think people who said things like, "everything happens for a reason" didn't know what the heck they were talking about. It would make me so angry whenever I heard those words or anything like them. I mean, who are they to tell me that there's a reason that I'm sitting in pain, or that my world is falling apart? What did *they* know?!

That was me, back in my twenty-somethings, thinking I was invincible, living by other people's standards and beliefs, being stuck in blame, judgment, guilt, and anger. I was constantly setting myself up for disappointment and heartache. I did these things unintentionally of course, but it was all I knew.

I grew up with the idea and belief that I had to be mean and aggressive to get the things I wanted in life and hold grudges against those who didn't see eye to eye with me or did me wrong. My world was so limited back then, but at the same time there was something deep inside of me that longed for love and kindness. It was strange, really: there I was, living my life, pretending to be happy and confident, when all I wanted to do was get away from it all and find something that was more fulfilling, a real purpose. Something pure, where I could just be me and be accepted for who I was without fear of judgment or disappointing others, especially the people I loved.

So why am I telling you this? Perhaps you can understand where I'm coming from and how I felt when I was living my life outside of my own genuine intentions. I was going against my intuition and ignoring it every step of the way as I made one bad decision after another.

We're human, and as humans we become conditioned to the stigmas of others around us as we grow up. It's up to us to fulfill our own lives with what *we* want, what we desire and what we want to create for ourselves. It wasn't until I got married to my first husband that I realized this and my true path.

The Nightmare

During the time leading up to our wedding, his parents separated. His father had moved out of the family home and rented an apartment in a nearby city. They were lovely people, and I got along well with them. I don't think his father was too keen on me, though, and being that I was still stuck in the mindset of taking things way too personally, I was always doubting people, including myself. My mother-in-law, however, is the sweetest, kindest person you could ever meet. Her zest for life was admirable, and after losing over a 100 pounds, she was more active and loved to travel. She had a cool, spiky short hairdo with blonde tips, fair skin and small, comforting brown eyes. I still had my doubts about her real feelings about me because I felt that she might have shared the same resistance that my father-in-law had about me, but of course I was still struggling with many insecurities and issues around self-esteem, trust, etc....

In short: I was a hot mess!

Not long after their separation, my mother-in-law began to form another romantic relationship with a high school sweetheart with whom she had reconnected on social media. My husband wasn't too thrilled with that idea and made it known to her on several occasions, and I backed him up on that 100%. We both felt that she needed to end things once and for all with my father-in-law before moving forward, but that wasn't our decision to make. She just wanted to be happy again.

One night, after many months of going back and forth on invitations to meet this new 'beau' in her life, we finally met them for dinner. It was just the four of us. It was a bit tense at first, sitting with them at the restaurant trying to make small talk when all my husband wanted to do was to be at home and stay out of it. He was a good sport and we all got through the night with nothing but respect and even a few laughs. I remember on the ride home that night, sharing that we both felt good seeing my mother-in-law happy again. And then we got home.

The phone was ringing as we walked through the door, and my husband made his way over to answer it (we had the ol' landline back then!). I was immediately attacked by our two cats, who wanted nothing but love and cuddles. As I made my way to the couch with the cats, I heard my husband say, "We'll be right there" and hung up the phone. He turned to me, very casually and calmly said that his mother had been shot in the head.

I sat there, frozen, heart in my stomach, not knowing what to say or even how to feel. I was in complete shock. He, on the other hand, was quite calm as I watched him gently grab the keys off the kitchen counter and say, "Let's go." I got up and followed him out the door, I don't even remember if I grabbed my purse or not. It was all a blur.

With some miraculous intervention, she survived. The bullet had lodged in the muscle of her left cheek, and it hadn't hit a bone! The surgeon was amazed and couldn't believe how lucky she was and how easy it was to remove the bullet. We were all so grateful and happy that she was going to be OK, outside of the emotional and mental anguish of course but that was something we could work through together.

Needless to say, there was so much more around this incident, but I'm saving that for another time. However, it's only fair to mention that yes, it was indeed my father-in-law who shot her, but that wasn't his only plan. Again, so much more to this part of my story, so stay tuned!

The Aftershock

So, there I was, newly married and processing the unfortunate circumstance between my in-laws. I was working as an administrative assistant at a pediatrics office, 4 years at this point, and I absolutely loved my work. I loved the people I worked with, all of the patients, and going into work every day in scrubs! It was nice that I didn't have to concern myself too much with wardrobe selection.

I was also an avid power walker in my spare time. I enjoyed being outside and getting fit. As a matter of fact, I was a member of the San Diego Fit team and trained for half marathons, in hopes that one day I would be able to power walk a full marathon (I wasn't much of a runner). I love sports of all kinds, but I actively participated in playing tennis and softball, both of which I played in high school (a long time ago!).

The day I noticed that my breath was slightly shallow, I was sitting on the couch, watching a movie. My chest felt a little tight and I thought it was a little strange because I wasn't moving or exerting myself in any way, but I didn't give it another thought and continued with my evening. Over the next several days, my breath was becoming more and more shortened, and an occasional tightness would overcome my chest. I mentioned it to my husband, and he suggested that it was probably the lack of exercise, as I had been slacking off from my walks and workouts. Yeah, he was probably right. I decided to get back on track and start my walks again the following day after work.

I was feeling rather sluggish when I got home that next day, but I pushed myself to get into my walking gear and get outside. I didn't get very far. I barely made it through the parking lot of our condominium complex to the main road when I suddenly couldn't catch my breath. I immediately turned around to head back home and I began to pay more attention to my body and what I was feeling. My chest was still tight, I felt a slight weakness, my breathing was heavy and an overwhelming fatigue came over me. It was then that it hit me: something was seriously wrong. I wasn't just out of shape. I tried to keep it together and just focus on getting back home. I literally wasn't sure if I was going to make it.

I made it home and I told my husband how I was feeling. He didn't seem too concerned and still chalked it up to being out of shape. I expressed to him that what I was feeling was very different, and I truly felt like something more intrusive was happening, but he didn't really understand. Neither of us said another word about it and continued to make dinner. I didn't have the energy to stay up and watch a movie that night so I went straight to bed. My body was feeling heavy, and my fatigue was growing by the minute. I thought I would wake up feeling better after 9-10 hours of sleep. The next morning came around and I was feeling 'meh' not really better but not much worse either. I went off to work as hard as it was to muster up the energy.

The day went OK, and we were busier than usual. Lots of paperwork to catch up on and the waiting room was a madhouse, filled with sick crying babies and restless kids with their panicked parents trying to patiently wait their turn. I noticed my strength beginning to weaken, especially as the day went on. There was one moment when I meant to hand some paperwork to a parent, but I couldn't get myself to reach her over the counter. She looked at me puzzled and asked if I was OK, and I embarrassingly said, "I don't know" as she reached down to meet me halfway.

As the day wound down and the last patients made their way home, I started to shut things down and clean up the waiting room of all the books and toys that were left on the floor. As I bent down to pick up the books, I placed them back on the bookshelf and went to stand back up. But I couldn't do it. I had literally lost all the strength in my legs. Panic set in and I was forced to face the realization of what was happening to me. It was time to confront what I had been afraid of, having no control of my body and wondering what could be taking over.

A nurse, and good friend, happened to walk by and saw the panic spreading across my face as I remained kneeling in the middle of the waiting room, alone. She ran over from behind the front office and helped me up. She was as shocked as I was and proceeded to take over my duties and send me home. She did her best in reassuring me that I was OK and to go home and get some rest. Her kindness warmed my heart and I held onto that as I made my way to the parking lot.

I got into my car and as I started to back up, I felt the weakness in my neck and the pain started to radiate as I tried to look back for oncoming traffic. As I drove out and started to make my way home, I realized that my entire body was feeling stiff, painful, hot, and it was hard to hold onto the steering wheel. It took so much energy to try and steer the car and I began to pray that He would get me home safely.

By the time I got home, I was a complete wreck. I could barely get my legs out of the car, I had to literally pull them up with my hands and even that was hard, as my arms were even weaker. My heart began to sink with fear, and I felt like falling to the ground in the fetal position and weeping myself out of this horrible nightmare. I persevered to the front door of my home, with every bit of energy I had in me, in a slow and barely manageable walk. My husband saw me through the window and immediately came to my aid at the front door. He, too, saw the panic in my face and hugged me so tight that the tears just started pouring down. I literally gave into the weakness as my husband helped me to the couch. He didn't know what to say or do, so he just sat with me and let me cry for a while.

After I was able to contain myself and breathe again, he helped me over to our bedroom and helped me get into my pajamas and into bed. Sleeping wasn't easy, I had a hard time trying to move my head from side to side and I had no strength to roll over by myself. The pain is what kept me up and even the maximum amount of over-the-counter pain medicine didn't make the slightest difference. My anxiety was too high, but I eventually got a few hours of sleep.

The next morning, it was a little harder to get out of bed, but I managed to do it, and to drag myself into the shower and get ready for work. It took all my might to get through my shower and my breath was extremely short and my heart was racing by the time I got out. I made my way back into the bedroom and sat on the side of my bed where my scrubs were laid out by my husband. I bent down, with panties in hand, and tried to pull them up my legs. Once again, I couldn't do it. My strength had depleted even more than the previous day. Something was seriously wrong, and panic set in all over again. I called my boss in tears and told her that I couldn't come into work because I had no strength to even get dressed, much less get in my car and drive. She was extremely concerned and offered me words of encouragement before making sure that my husband called the doctor for me. The pain was indescribable. People often asked me if it's like muscle soreness from a hard workout, as they would try and understand what I was feeling, but it was a pain that I could never imagine or describe. The best I could do: it's like a very deep bone chill, a constant sharp ache that never goes away.

I remember having to wait a few days before my appointment, and it felt like an eternity. I was scared beyond belief, not knowing whether I was going to make it through whatever this was, or even worse, if it would take my life. If you have ever been in this sort of situation, then I trust that you can empathize with my worry and fear. It's the worst part of disease, having to wait for a diagnosis, and hoping that there is one. You start to play back everything you've done in your life that could have possibly triggered this unforeseeable reaction and pain. What could I have done wrong? It began to take me over mentally, and I was an emotional wreck. I'm sure this didn't help my situation, but I didn't know any better, all I knew was that I couldn't move a single limb or walk very well.

My husband took time off from work to stay home with me the first month, as I needed physical help getting out of bed, going to the bathroom, and making my meals. I had already gone through three appointments with my primary care doctor, whom I had never met before. There was never a reason to go visit her until now. She was a young, beautiful and stylish doctor, probably straight out of med school. She wasn't very attentive to my husband's concerns, and she was very dismissive. On the third visit, I was in my worst form. I could barely walk or lift my arms, and I could barely lift my head up. I was in so much pain, from head to toe, and it was constant. Thank goodness my husband was there to advocate for me, he was my voice and made sure that I was taken care of.

I was diagnosed about four months later, by which time I was already confined to a wheelchair. The pain was always there, and I remember spending many days crying, wondering if I was ever going to be free from the pain and walk again.

I was diagnosed with Dermatomyositis (DM), a rare autoimmune disease that depletes muscle activity. In general, myositis is inflammation that surrounds the muscles and prevents mobility. It causes prolonged muscle fatigue, weakness and pain. My specific form of myositis also affects my skin, leaving me with a papule-like rash around my face and joints. It's not curable, like most autoimmune diseases, but it can be managed.

Although it was a scary disease to me because I'd never heard of it before (heck, I wasn't even sure if I could spell it!) I was happy to at least know that there was a name for it. Once I was able to wrap my head around it and talk to my doctors about a treatment plan, I was able to see some glimmers of hope.

As I began to respond, finally, to the treatments after several months, I was in a completely different space emotionally, spiritually, and obviously physically. I was, and still am, filled with so much gratitude that I was able to overcome this rare disease and acquire full remission. With the help and encouragement of my physical therapist, with whom I worked for two years, I was able to get out of my wheelchair and slowly regain my strength and balance. I was able to retrieve my confidence and stride and most importantly my muscle activity.

Unfortunately, my marriage did not make it through all of this, and we amicably went our separate ways not long after my recovery. I am grateful, though, that I was given such a wonderful person who cared for me, loved me and guided me through such a difficult time. I truly believe that we are handed just what we need at the right time. There is not one day that I don't hold gratitude for him and for all the other friends and people who were there for me. I also hold peace for those who weren't there for me, the ones who I thought would be front and center, but never showed up.

The Light

Going through this difficult and dark period in my life has triggered more than just awareness around my physical wellbeing and how important it is to pay more attention to my body, but it also opened the windows that I had always known were there but just didn't know how to find them.

This entire process of trauma, my illness, and my recovery has taught me how to become more self-aware and present with everything that I face in my life. It was just what I needed to humble my soul and guide me in a better, more fulfilling direction. It has led me to a beautiful life through mindfulness.

I have learned so many lessons through these experiences, like paying more attention to my body and listening to the messages that it sends me. I no longer chalk off certain symptoms or feelings as easily as I used to. I have learned to take the time to sit back and really feel what's coming up, whether it's a physical symptom or emotional one. I allow it to be there and get curious as to why it's showing up. What does my body need me to do to recover, why am I having this thought? I am now able to connect with myself on a much deeper level and avoid the drama that my mind used to create. We've all done it, made assumptions about people or situations and created stories that give us anxiety, anger or sadness.

Learning how to release what I can't control was another impactful lesson hidden in the dark realms of my DM. I was forced to realize the power of 'one day at a time,' a phrase that my late mother always told us kids. A phrase that I took for granted and would shrug off with, *"yeah, yeah."* I now get, and feel, the power of letting go and staying within each moment, through the pain, worry, and fear, acknowledging the little wins I made with each new day. As hard as it was to release my worries and fears, I learned that by trying every day, I began to feel much calmer and more at ease. I've been able to open up the space that I needed to see things more clearly and with more compassion.

Accepting what is and asking for help, I learned how to let go of my pride and embarrassment and let others do for me. This wasn't easy, but I really had no choice. I couldn't move, much less do any of the daily things that were most intimate, such as going to the bathroom or taking a shower. I needed help in areas of my life that were most vulnerable. This is when we have to accept our reality, lean on others, and trust in the process. Trust yourself to be taken care of by those who are willing and caring enough to help. Through these experiences we can begin to feel things like shame and guilt, but if you don't learn how to let these feelings go you will only stay stuck in a mindset that can jeopardize your mental health.

Cultivating patience for myself and with others was another lesson I learned. I was always moving so quickly through life, getting everything done and not even thinking twice about it. If someone needed me, I was there. If I had a deadline, I got it done. I rarely said "no" to those who asked for my help, and when I did, I let myself feel guilty and wallow in the speculations of what others might have thought about me. I was a people pleaser by far.

By going through my bout with DM, I quickly learned how to slow down and give myself the time and set the boundaries I needed through my healing process. It was extremely hard, but when I started to learn more about mindfulness and the practices that have given me personal and emotional freedom, things became much clearer in terms of what's important to me. I had to learn to say "no" and be patient with myself and with my healing process. These things can't be rushed. It doesn't happen overnight and most certainly won't change if we don't have patience and compassion for ourselves.

I guess I could say, like many others who have been challenged by chronic pain, that my illness led me to the place that I always knew was there waiting. A place where I can work through my own faults, insecurities and thoughts that kept me stuck in scarcity and fear. It was a fierce wake-up call, and yes, I had to face my own mortality and go through the dark before I was able to recognize my own power.

Just as the alcoholic must hit 'rock bottom' to see their potential and live a more fruitful and intentional life, I too had to hit my own rock bottom to do just the same. It's a life journey as I am always evolving and changing, just like you and all the world. I must remember that with evolution comes adaptation and that focusing on the here and now is the key to creating what I want to create.

I've since gone on to educate myself on a holistic journey to live a more intentional life through preventative, functional medicine. I received my license as a holistic health practitioner in 2005 and have been helping others do the same through mindfulness practice and other holistic modalities. I'm a firm believer of mind over body and that we have complete control of how our lives and wellbeing thrive.

As life keeps me on my toes through all its trials and tribulations, I am getting better every day at being more aware of my thoughts, responsibilities, and reactions. I can focus on what really matters like my happiness, wellness and peace of mind and move through it with more ease and grace.

This is what I hope for you as well. I hope that you, too, find the space to pay more attention to your own thoughts and intentions and how they affect your life. I hope that you can give yourself the love and patience that you deserve. It's not easy navigating through life, especially in today's world, and when you have loved ones to care for it's important to seek the guidance and support that you need to help you show up and continue to create a better version of *you* with each new day. You are never alone, and please remember: everything you do, say, and create matters.

As I have evolved over the years since my remission, I have become a holistic health practitioner and dedicated my energy to living a more intentional life through mindfulness practice. Now, I dedicate my energy and focus on helping others through their darkness so that they can embrace their own challenges with more confidence, ease and most importantly their own truth.

I want my clients to live by what matters to them, and only them, without any fears or doubt because we ALL deserve to live our truth.

ANGELIC INGRAM
ABOUT THE AUTHOR

Angelic Ingram is a Holistic Health Practitioner, mindfulness coach, and author. Through her own journey of adversity and life experiences, she is passionate about guiding her clients to attain inner peace, happiness and success with her signature mindfulness program. Angelic loves to travel with her husband, read and write inspiring stories, volunteer, watch sports, cuddle with dogs and eat nachos! She also volunteers with the Myositis Support and Understanding organization where she moderates mindfulness conversations on clubhouse, among other projects, and advocates for myositis awareness and other rare chronic diseases that have also affected her life.

www.linktr.ee/mindfuljourneytofreedom

6

FINDING GRACE

DISCOVERING MYSELF THROUGH HEARTBREAK, LOSS & SUCCESS

By Mary Gouganovski

Total *devastation.*

That's the only way I can describe what I saw and felt as I surveyed the damage. Everything I and my family had worked so hard to build for the last fifteen years, reduced to a pile of debris.

They say women are like tea, you never know how strong we are until we're dropped into hot water. I couldn't agree more. For years, I felt like I was so deep in that water, I was drowning in it. A vast and raging ocean that battered me from all sides, pushing me deeper and deeper until I could no longer see the light filtering through on the surface. I couldn't breathe, I was screaming for the ocean to let me out, to save me - but the ocean couldn't hear me, *it didn't care.*

Every time I looked at my feet, I found anchors. They just kept attaching. Tethers binding me to the ocean floor, pulling me under, and the more desperately I tried to kick them off, the faster I drowned. Every day felt like a battle, like the life force of my very existence had been drained from me... and the next day, I'd do it all again.

Yet, we persevere. Why? because we have to. Because what other choice do we have?

At least, that's how it feels.

I have been in business my entire life, it's all I've ever known. For twenty years, I have been immersed in this world. Starting as a humble family business, a little shop in a tiny country town in New South Wales, Australia. Our first Christmas, we were blessed to have customers pouring in, and every day, I'd work the register. I was so small, I couldn't see over the counter.

My anxiety started back then...

"Mumma, how are we going to handle all of these people?" I asked, wide eyed as my gaze flickered desperately between her loving face and the door. "It's okay baby, you just stand there and serve them, one customer at a time," she said to me as she put a little stool by the register so I could stand tall enough to see everything I needed to see.

And see, I did.

We built that little 100 square metre shop with everything we had, and ran it successfully for fifteen incredibly long years, working seven days a week, twelve hours a day.

We handled everything that came our way with exactly the same mentality: one obstacle at a time. Until the hits kept coming so hard and so fast, I found myself in that water... only this time, I didn't have a stool to get up. I had no way out.

We lost our shop in torrential floods in 2016. An entire town—homes, landmarks and over 60 businesses—were gone in just a few hours. It was one of the most terrifying experiences of my life, and as we gutted our humble little shop the following day and stood in the empty shell that used to contain our whole world, we knew that nothing would ever be the same again.

Change is good, it's great. It's what we all need to move forward in life. But not all change is easy, and often when you're going through it, you wonder how you'll ever be the same again. Will things ever return to normal? What is normal?

Even though we had our factory, it took my mum a year to pick herself up from that loss, and in a way, I think we're still trying to pick up the pieces...

Before I delve any deeper into this story, let's rewind 20 years. My name is Mary Gouganovski, I'm a young entrepreneur from a small country town in the Southern Highlands, NSW. I grew up in the family business.

Armed with nothing but a credit card and sheer force of will, my mum and brother started a boutique gift, candles and jewellery store. It had become such a well known shop, and its presence touched so many lives. Mum filled it with beautiful things she adored, and it was one of the few places at the time that focused on purely Australian-made candles. I would spend every afternoon, weekend and holiday there.

A few years in, the Global Financial Crisis hit and we lost countless suppliers within months of each other. Our customers were desperate for two fragrances that had been so popular at the time but we couldn't source anywhere; rose and chocolate. Despite the recession, we were able to cling on, and decided to fill that very need. Within weeks, we had begun wholesaling, and months after that, we held the keys to our very first factory unit. Contract manufacturing came not long after and before we knew it, we'd built an empire out of wax and wick... though at its core, the shop remained. It had become our entire life for so long that watching it wash away was, to this day, one of the hardest things we've ever endured.

Standing in the remnants of our life, I sobbed at the loss before shutting the doors one last time. The real grief came later, the mourning of a life that once was. What next? How would we rebuild?

The following year passed in a blur, moving in a monotonous haze as we picked up the pieces. When we decided to focus purely on the factory, on our brand and manufacturing arm, I knew then that we had to pivot once more. It was time to change, and the first step was separating our brand from our shop and our company. I knew that was our future, the only way we'd really move forward, but the family wasn't quite ready to let it go. The name, Endless Candles, was so personal to us all, and whilst it wasn't truly being let go, that separation of a name that defined a beloved home was still too soon, too raw. Salt on a bitter wound.

So another year passed as I continued to tread that water. I felt so lost. You always hear about people's success, and for most on the outside, it always seems like it's overnight. A brand, a figure, a thing, whatever it may be; invisible one day and unavoidable the next. What you don't see is the countless hours, days, months, years that went on behind the scenes. The blood, sweat and tears that went into the process until it finally became a tangible thing.

No one talks about it. Not really. They brush over it, touching light as a feather on the hardship they endured and the sheer force of will it took to climb their way to the top, but even more so, what they had to do to stay there. It's not a steady ride, there's always ups and downs. Two steps forward, three steps back.

I want you to know the truth, that the only place that success comes before work is in the dictionary. It's not to fear it, but to help you prepare. May my story, like so many others, inspire you, prepare you for the journey you're about to face. Whether that's in business or in life.

I could tell you the first secret to success. It's one single word... are you ready? Are you sitting down? It's mind blowing, the kind of thing that'll change your entire perspective on everything I'm about to tell you.

The secret is **passion**.

It's amazing, I know. Such a shock to the system, but honestly - in business, in life, in any situation - passion is your singular driving force. It doesn't matter whether that's for a brand, a product, to make money, to become well known, to start a relationship, to end a relationship - if you're not passionate about what you're doing, or what you want to achieve then it's not the right thing for you.

With passion comes drive, determination, the super strength to pick yourself up after a heartache or loss and continue treading water until land appears.

I knew, in one form or another, that I wanted to be here. Right now. I knew that I wanted to create an empire, a brand that would touch the hearts and souls of countless people. Whether they're customers, or just part of the Mary Grace family. I knew that I wanted to develop a range of products, from skincare and bath and body to home fragrance and the like, that was beautiful, luxurious, safe and affordable. That anyone, especially the most sensitive, could use. I knew I wanted to stand tall and proud, and build a community of like-minded people who could bond over a shared need, who could find a place where they felt seen, heard, and acknowledged. A place where they could belong. A place where I could belong, too.

What I didn't know was how the heck I'd get there. I couldn't tell you what that looked like, in fact for two years after the loss of our shop, I floated along in that ocean, trying to find a way out, but everywhere I turned there was simply more water... Until one day, my mum walked into my office and said, "Mary, I think we need to change the name of our brand."

"Yes!" I screamed, fist pumping the air like a child at Christmas.

I couldn't help it. I'd been *waiting* for this moment for so long, yearning for a day in which my family would be ready to accept the next step. Endless Candles was beautiful, still is, the name stands tall and proud across the front of our building. It's the backbone of who we are. But it limited me, left me with no room to grow, no way to find the path I needed to step onto to realise my dreams.

It wasn't just me who thought so.

If you want the most brutal feedback about your brand, exhibit at a trade show. They don't hold back! People would walk past our stand, see our name printed in great big letters across the front of the display, and mutter "Candles? More bloody candles, I'm sick to death of them!" Those two simple words were enough to prevent a person from lifting their gaze 6 inches to a glorious display of products.

And so, Mary Grace was finally born.

The name came to me within ten minutes of mum walking into my office. It was the second one we chose, and it was truly perfect. I looked it up, and everything was available! Not just available, but begging me to take it. I'd changed our brand within an hour. Website, domains, logo, social media: the whole kit and kaboodle. I spent several days fielding calls from long-time customers wondering what on earth was going on, all the while floating in a cloud of giddiness from the change. I knew this was the right choice, and sure enough, by the next trade show the tone of people walking past was different. "Mary Grace, what a pretty name."

I was in the midst of working out what I wanted to do with my newfound freedom, trying to decide what product lines to introduce and how I wanted to position myself now, when my grandmother got sick.

Two Steps Forward, Three Steps Back

I didn't know it then, but it was the beginning of the end for her. My beautiful, stoic grandmother who had the haunting eyes of an ocean amidst a raging storm, who had escaped war and poverty to single-handedly build a better life for her children, who had been there without question for 27 years, was fine one day and confined to a hospital bed the next. We were with her every day for eight months. Two in the hospital, six at home. I continued with the business the best I could, an hour and a half away from home whilst nursing her back to health.

She couldn't speak English very well, nor I Macedonian. I was fluent as a little girl, but that lost language fell to the wayside as I started school. But when she came home, and a little colour returned to her cheeks, I'd lay with her in bed and we'd watch reruns of Frasier, Becker, The Nanny... and she'd laugh at the screen, pointing out different things that she'd see. She started to open up to me about her life back in her village, her sister and brothers. She was orphaned at eight years old, and hadn't seen her siblings in over fourty years.

We'd just returned to work, our first trade show since she'd gotten sick. Truly thinking she was getting better; the only reason we left to exhibit at the show. Her last words to me before I left her still haunt me. "Don't worry, I'll wait for you." And she did. She waited for us to board our flights home before ending up in that hospital bed again, waited for all of us to be by her bedside before falling into a catatonic state, and four days later... she was gone. Falling back into the arms of all those who'd come before her.

There was no time to mourn, with her funeral followed by another trade show a week later, I had to pick up the pieces of my heart and move forward.

We were already dealing with so much, and for the most part, I was numb to the pain... but my Grandmother taught me so many life lessons. She had crossed the world with two young children, survived war, health battles, a new country with an intense language barrier - and she did it all on her own. Creating a life for her family out of resilient stoicism. She never gave up, despite the loneliness and sacrifice, despite the heart ache. Fighting like a true warrior until her final breath.

She reminded me what it means to fight for what you love. To fight for a better life. I had already come so far, I couldn't give up now. It was bigger than me, I knew that. So I picked up the next building block, pushing harder every day.

I launched four new product lines within three months of the name change, and spent another year really honing those lines. Deciding how I wanted them to look, what products, what value I wanted to offer. How I wanted to position Mary Grace within a wide and beautiful market.

Despite what I foresaw, however, the tide continued to ebb and flow. My grand plans shifted and changed constantly. Had I fought it, like in the beginning, I'm certain I'd have drowned.

My idea of a perfect range or a perfect business changed so often I gave myself a headspin. But it wasn't just me, the world was changing dramatically. Whilst my own life had stood still for those eight months, something else was lurking around the corner.

Soon, fire ravaged our land.

The worst bushfires we'd seen in - I couldn't even tell you how long - threatened to tear apart everything we'd worked for. We spent three months sandwiched between two out of three of the largest and most dangerous fires in New South Wales. Kept safe merely by the way the wind blew.

Three months of living in fear: watching, waiting, listening. Would today be the day? The Green Wattle Creek fire was just on the other side of a small, narrow bridge. Separating that blaze from a factory finally restocked with all the products I had been so desperately needing to replace whilst taking care of my grandmother.

New Year's Eve was spent listening to the sirens of the fire brigade, patrolling the streets of my tiny neighbourhood as the sky turned orange, then a deep red. Ash fell to the ground, staining our world with reminders of what was coming. On high alert for evacuation, until it was too late to leave... An entire state in turmoil until the call came to say the fires had been subdued, eventually beaten. That call came weeks later.

Collectively, we breathed a sigh of relief. For what felt like a single moment in time.

And then, the pandemic hit.

It was all so surreal. How could we possibly work through this, too? How are we expected to take the hits and get up *every single time?* It felt like an impossible task. Our doors were closed, our staff sent home, our future uncertain. For the fourth time in four years, I thought: this is it, the moment that will finally break me.

And then I learnt the second secret to success. You'd think it would have come to me sooner, such a blatantly obvious thing I don't know why it isn't being shouted across rooftops or sprawled along billboards. Perhaps it is, perhaps I wasn't ready to hear it before now. Too stuck in what I *thought* was the path I should have been on to reach my end destination. But there, solid as a rock, the realisation struck me in the face.

Are you ready?

Reinvention

It's key, just ask Madonna. The only way to stay relevant, to stay *in the now* whilst continuing to drive forward, is to learn how to reinvent yourself. To learn how to pivot. I'm sure after two and a half years of this pandemic you're sick of hearing the word pivot, but I'm here to tell you it's important. Because that word doesn't only save your sweet behind when the world is backed into a corner. Sometimes, learning how to pivot is the thing that keeps you afloat, even on the best of days.

In hindsight (I know, everything looks amazing under the light of hindsight), I had been pivoting all along. A seasoned professional by the time I'd reached this point - but going with the flow and letting the business drive me forward, not the other way around, had been the ultimate saving grace.

We were four days into our shut-down when we landed a sanitiser job with government approvals to not only reopen and operate but make and distribute the product to homes in need and frontline workers. Being in a small country town, it was an opportunity hard to come by. Something that was absolutely irrelevant to our regular day to day. I didn't know the first thing about sanitiser, or how to fill it. We were still very green to our liquid-filling side at the time, having only ever made diffusers and room sprays previously, but I was determined to work it out.

We partnered with two other small businesses, a distillery in Cowra who provided the base and a distributor in Albury. Two other NSW towns that had been tragically affected by the same fire we had been. I came up with the name for our offering almost as soon as the other two companies had come on board: Vintage 66. Named after the 66 employees who were able to keep their jobs, and continue working as we made the product.

The next day, we were able to make the calls to our staff that they could come back to work.

For a month, we worked tirelessly on producing the sanitiser. Over 9,000 bottles made it to people in need, and it was just enough to keep us afloat until things started to open back up again.

The job terrified me. It was so far out of my comfort zone, out of our normal repertoire of work, that every bone in my body was screaming at me to back out... but I couldn't. The fate of our business, our livelihoods relied on us finding a way to keep moving forward. That phrase, it seemed, was the one I was destined to chant to the beat of my drum. You can't ever stop... and so I did my due diligence, all my research, and obtained the approvals we needed to keep going.

Had I closed the door on that opportunity out of the fear that sat squarely on my chest, threatening to push me down, I'm honestly not sure I'd be sitting here right now, writing this.

We wouldn't have made it, and my story wouldn't have been one of success.

Stepping out of my comfort zone was the third secret to success, and arguably, one of the hardest.

It's the one you really have to dig deep for, push yourself to greater limits to achieve. It doesn't always come naturally, it's not ingrained in your psyche, it's not something you can just teach yourself. It's the most turbulent of all the secrets, and something I struggle with to this day. Every morning, I have to remind myself of why I do what I do, and why it's important to not just go the extra mile, but lap the whole damn universe.

In the height of the pandemic, and on the day of my 28th birthday, I received my first purchase order from the biggest thing that would happen to my brand, to date.

TVSN.

Australia's Television Shopping Network. They had remodelled their shows over the last decade to feature the best and most luxurious brands from across the world, and had chosen *me*. Mary Grace. I sent an email throwing my hat in the ring, (because you've *always* got to be in it to win it, a little side secret there) and 9 months later, I received a reply. It took another 9 months to onboard me, amongst a myriad of screening tests and being able to prove that, as a young woman, I'd still fit amongst their audience and do well on screen. By July, I was on air. Live. With absolutely no idea what the heck I was doing.

It was the most intimidating moment of my life.

My very first day on the show, I was given the chance to feature in their Good Morning TVSN segment, the live hour that showcases the brands that'll be on air for the day. It was a five minute window, prior to my hour-long show later that afternoon.

It was there that I came face to face with the biggest hurdle in my career to that point. Turns out, it had little to do with my brand, and everything to do with my mindset.

Stepping onto the set, there were 3 giant cameras, remotely manned. It felt like they were 7ft tall the way they towered over me, followed by a giant TV showing everything the cameras see at the same time as well as the audience, floor staff, the presenter and myself.

Despite all the chaos, all I could see?

Was me.

Having to sit on a beautiful couch, next to an even more beautiful presenter, and all I could think about was… why did I choose to wear a navy shirt? Do you remember Violet Beauregarde from Willy Wonka, when she turned into that giant blueberry? That's exactly how I felt.

I was live on international television, and I wanted to cry.

I remember sending emails to the producer after that begging her to let me stand, let me hide behind the display counter rather than sitting on a couch or a stool.

The Devil is in the Mirror

As a young European woman, I've struggled with my weight, my body and my mind my entire life. It started in my teens. I was feeling depressed and angry, my panic attacks growing more severe as the months flew by. I started feeling suicidal around the age of 18. I would cry to my mum, visiting doctor after doctor, trying to figure out the cause of my emotions. I knew I needed help, or I'd end up doing something I couldn't come back from. And I had no idea *why*.

Every doctor we visited would focus on my weight. Despite me telling them that my metabolism was sluggish, that I could hardly handle the sight of food let alone eat it, all they'd focus on was my size. "You're depressed because you're fat." "Make sure you count *all* the calories, even the incidental ones." "Are you sure you don't sleep-eat?" "Do you want to consider weight loss surgery?" You name it, I heard it.

It took a few more years before I found a doctor willing to *really* listen. Finally, I had an answer. Diagnosed at 20 years old with Insulin Resistance so severe I was told I wouldn't make it to my 25th birthday. It's an auto-immune disease that sits on the same spectrum as diabetes, just on the opposite end. Where a diabetic needs insulin, my brain doesn't recognize that my pancreas makes it, so it just keeps making more.

By the time I was diagnosed, the IR had shut down vital systems in my body and started attacking the part of my brain that affected my emotions... which explained my depression. I remember sitting in the doctor's office all alone, and being told that if he wasn't able to help lower the levels within six months, I wouldn't make it to my 25th birthday.

The closer I got to thirty, the worse my weight got, and the harder my panic attacks hit. And every time I received my show hours, the part of me that had worked tirelessly day in and day out to be here was incredibly proud of what I had accomplished... but the emotional side of me, the side that had been bullied her entire life for her weight, for her heritage, for her braces, for... you name it... winced at the thought of being seen.

There's still a video of me doing a live Q&A on facebook, and I was so panicked, felt so overweight sitting in that chair, that I could hardly talk, struggled to breathe, and just wanted *out*.

Stepping out of my comfort zone is something I have to reteach myself. Every. Single. Day. It's taken me two whole years to be comfortable enough in my own skin to stand in front of a camera, though I still need to fight back the part of me that begs me to run and hide, that shies away from people's words.

I started a daily gratitude journal, writing down one thing I was thankful for about myself, my life, my work - anything I felt disconnected from that day. I kept a second journal writing thoughts, feelings and affirmations that came to me. Some days, well, every day in the beginning, my words were very much a *fake it 'till you make it* scenario, but after a while I really started to believe what I'd write. I still have moments when I get in my head but writing my emotions helped me begin to process them. Going out, I'd look around and realise - no one else cared how I looked. It was only me, judging myself so much I felt unworthy of... *everything*.

It's only when you're really willing to *climb*, even when your lungs are burning and your limbs are shaking and you feel like you couldn't possibly take the next rung on that ladder and really *pull yourself up* that you'll truly realise your own strength.

You do the impossible every single day, we just forget that in the chaos of life.

Which brings me to my final secret; **learning to rely on yourself.**

I've had to learn to rely on myself more times than I can count. Shakespear wrote; "Uneasy lies the head that wears a crown", and I really couldn't agree more. It's so lonely here, trying to run an empire and do it all. You're never alone, not completely, but you'll find out fast who your friends are, who respects your business or your passion and understands the sacrifice needed to get through those hurdles. Don't wait for rescue: pull yourself out of that ocean and find dry land.

Growing up, my mum always said to me "knowledge is power." She'd tell me my word is my wand, and the pen was always mightier than the sword. You might roll your eyes at the cliche, but boy oh boy was she right. The day you stop learning is the day you die. It's important to know absolutely every aspect of your business, from start to finish. You can outsource, because we can't always be everything but if you don't know what you're outsourcing, how do you know you're not being fooled?

There's a running joke that someone who's the jack of all trades, is the master of none... but that's not the full phrase. Shakespeare wrote, "a jack of all trades is a master of none, but oftentimes better than a master of one." It's one of the most powerful secrets you need to conquer your dreams.

I've made it my mission to learn everything about Mary Grace. For the moment, I do it all, too. From graphic design, range creation, product development, web design, social media, IT, manufacturing... and despite my Bachelors Degree, I'm self taught in it all. I've started to outsource some parts of my business now, because the burnout has finally started to rear its ugly head... but, aside from all the money I've saved, my knowledge and skill mean that someone has to get up incredibly early to pull the wool over my eyes.

With Floods, Come the Ark

A wise friend said to me; "you're never completely out of adversity," and I couldn't agree more. I've found over the course of my life that I've always been treading water in that vast ocean. It's a constant battle of sink or swim. Every time I think *something's just got to give, life has to get easier,* another wave crashes over me, forcing me back down. That feeling of drowning, suffocating and inescapable, all consuming. I think we just get better at dealing with the hurdles. Eventually, we push through until we breach the surface. We find a way to start building an ark amidst that raging sea, giving us hope, something to cling on to.

It's through every moment of adversity that I was able to experience the life lessons that gave me the knowledge to build that ark, until I stood atop an empire that could withstand the waves. I look back at the generations of women who came before me, and all that they have endured. I look to the women surrounding me now, to you, reading these pages and take solace in knowing that I wasn't alone. That through everything I have endured, I'm still here, still fighting- and you are too.

Everything I've done in my life has brought me to this point. To grow, adapt and evolve as life does. I am constantly learning, to enhance and grow my skills, my brand, my mindset... everything I do, I circle back to step one. *Passion.*

Just ask yourself this; how badly do you want to take the next step? Whether you can see where your foot lands or not; if you want something desperately enough, what will you do to fight for it? It's okay to feel worried or scared, our path has already been forged.

Trust in that journey, and if you feel lost, alone or in need of a friend, know that you'll always find one within the pages of this book.

MARY GOUGANOVSKI

ABOUT THE AUTHOR

Mary Gouganovski is the founder & director of Mary Grace, an award-winning Australian beauty and lifestyle brand specialising in natural, sustainable, ethical, and cruelty-free formulations for the face, body, and home. Starting out in the family's beloved small-town candle boutique over twenty years ago, Mary developed a work ethic at a very young age and found passion in the day-to-day challenges and triumphs of entrepreneurship. She holds a Bachelor in Business and Commerce Majoring in Marketing, a Certificate 4 in Small Business Management and a Diploma in Copywriting. Currently residing in the southern highlands of NSW, Mary is a self-taught entrepreneur, community advocate, and budding motivational voice.

In her spare time, she enjoys books and movies, is in the process of writing a fantasy novel, and functions on coffee and adrenaline. She loves Autumn and Winter, daylight savings and lazy Sunday mornings.

www.marygouganovski.com

7

MAKING FRIENDS WITH SHAME

By Erica Tatum-Sheade

My hands felt like ice. My stomach churned. My face burned with red-hot shame. All I wanted in that moment was to disappear, but it felt like a glaring spotlight was shining directly in my face. All eyes were on me as I took a deep breath, swallowed hard, and finally managed to force my dry mouth to form the words: "John 3:16."

But perhaps we should rewind a bit.

My name is Erica Tatum-Sheade. At one point, saying those words was probably one of the most difficult tasks you could have assigned to me. To say that I was shy is an understatement: I had no voice, and had been engineering myself to stay small and quiet, choosing not to make waves or bring attention to myself.

The choice to have a voice was stolen from me early in life. I didn't quite understand it at the time, but I had allowed a "friend" to move in and rob me of my voice. I call this a "friend" because at first, I felt it was there to protect me, to keep me safe. This *friend* first arrived when I was 8 years old. I was small and felt helpless and weak in relation to the events happening around me. It whispered to me "just stay quiet and things will be okay." I initially found solace in this, I could be safe this way – but the more I allowed this *friend* to take over, the more I disappeared. It stole my voice, my joy, and the very essence that made me, *me*.

What I know now, as an adult and a licensed therapist, is that the messages we hear and see shape how we see ourselves, especially in those early years of development. Whenever I am speaking on building self-esteem with our girls I say, "Eight is great, but nine ain't so fine." Around age nine, we start to experience hits to our self-esteem and self-confidence. Those with whom we surround ourselves start to influence the reflection we see of ourselves.

For me, what that looked like was that all of a sudden this *friend*, that little voice, would say these things to me: "*You're not like other girls,*" "*Nobody cares about you,*" "*Do you really think you're smart enough,*" "*You're not pretty enough,*" "*You're too different.*"

It started as a whisper, but things kept happening to reinforce it. Every time I didn't get invited to a birthday party, that voice would get louder: "*Nobody wants to be your friend.*" Any time I felt like I didn't do well on something: "*You're too stupid to be successful.*" When I tried to speak, but wasn't heard: "*No one understands you.*" That voice that started as a whisper just got louder and louder and louder...

I stopped showing up, and the voice, that *friend,* had started to show up in place of me. It caused disconnection in my friendships, it affected my relationships, it affected how I related to my family, and it affected my faith. It would have me questioning things, thinking: "*If my family really cared about me, they would listen to me; if I really was a good person, people would want to be my friend. If God truly loved me, he wouldn't let these things keep happening to me.*"

Eventually, I just stopped existing. Allowing this voice to speak for me, I created what I call a "shame bubble" around me. I wouldn't show up, my shame would show up in place of me. How I interacted with people was based on the shame that I was feeling, it was based on the story that I was telling myself.

Walking into a room, I wasn't walking into a room full of possibilities, I was walking into a room telling myself, "*They don't care about you, they don't like you."* I was going through the motions, but never truly experiencing the life I deserved. I was limiting myself out of fear and out of shame.

That voice was with me at 8, at 19, and at 24. I thought I could outrun it; if I did all the things and checked all the boxes, I would be okay, I would be thriving. So I did just that, believing the hype that if you just did things that successful, happy people did, then you, too, could be successful and happy. Trying to outrun the *friend*, the voice that I had invited to live inside my head all those years ago, the voice that I had given permission to speak for me? Well, that wasn't going to be that easy.

I often speak of the "pivot moments," those moments when I had to go to battle with my shame in order to pivot, to free myself from what had been holding me back. The first was the birth of my first child. I had been in this constant battle of questioning my worthiness: as a wife, as a mother, and as a woman. I had already given up on the notion that I could have good, healthy friendships, because I had decided that I was not worthy of those connections. I had already put all of these labels on myself of who I thought I was based on my own shame talk.

I remember sitting there, holding this child that I was now supposed to be responsible for, and absolutely FREAKING OUT. That was the moment that I knew something had to change, and so I tried to lean into what I knew. What I knew was that, deep down in their core, the people who feel that they are worthy are the people who have strong connections. So, I joined all sorts of clubs. Moms' clubs, couples clubs, new graduates Clubs, brunch clubs... you name it. I knew I needed a village; I needed somebody to see me, I needed validation, I needed someone to tell me that I was OK and that I was acceptable – but that didn't happen. I describe what happened like this: it was just like what happens for those of us that have iPhones and we opt to get the cheap charger instead of the $40 Apple charger. You plug it in, and there on the screen it says: **"this accessory not supported by this phone."**

I was experiencing a series of "misconnections," because I still wasn't showing up! I was still allowing my shame to show up for me. That voice was still in my head: "*these people don't like you, look at them you're so different.*" Some of these messages I even got directly from the very people I was trying to connect with, because they weren't all "my people." It just kept reiterating that same shame story that I had been holding on to since I was 8 years old, sometimes yelling it: "*YOU ARE NOT WORTHY.*" Just like when I was 8 years old, I started to retreat, going deeper into the void, trying not to exist.

At this point in my life, I had started my career and was doing what I call "hearts work," working with children and families supporting them through difficult times. The voices of the children are what stuck with me the most. Most social workers can tell you the cases that stick with them, the cases that push us deeper into our values and our commitment to the field. We can also tell you the ones that break us, and leave us struggling to sleep at night. Doing this work helped me to understand that shame can no longer live here. Shame keeps us suffering in silence, it stops us from becoming the best version of ourselves, it leaves us empty and alone. I knew that I couldn't continue on this road. I couldn't empower clients if I wasn't empowering myself.

The second occurrence of facing my shame happened just a few years ago, in my late 30's. I had taken this class at our church that was basically to help you get a deeper understanding of faith. In this class, we were learning about the history of the church, following Jesus from birth to death. I showed up for the first class, stepped in the room, and two things happened: one, I was the only brown face in the room (which tends to happen quite often for me, as I live in an area where there aren't a lot of people who look like me). Shame stepped in the room with me and immediately said, "*These people don't look like you, do you really think you can be vulnerable in this room? Do you think you are safe here?*" The second thing that happened was that I immediately noticed that I was the youngest person in the room by about 20 years; this was apparently the "seniors" group. Right on cue, there was shame reminding me this is another place where I don't belong, another place where I don't get to exist.

I had to make a quick decision. Instead of letting shame win, and shrinking as I had so many times before, I said to it, "Not today, I'm gonna ride this out and just see where it goes." And I did! I continued to show up, but I made a point to sit in my little corner and hope that nobody interacted with me. Though this was a slightly different version of my misconnections from the past, I remained open to SOMETHING, anything that might help me to make the change I so desperately wanted for myself. Sitting in my corner, staying small worked. Until one day, when we were going around and everybody was sharing their favorite story or verse from the bible. People were sharing some really profound things and verses that I had never even heard, and I was silently pleading for time to speed up so I didn't have to share. There was one particular person in class who would talk for half an hour if you let them, and I was crossing my fingers that they would be called on before me.

One thing we learn when facing the obstacles placed in front of us: there is never an easy way out, and of course the Universe always has other plans for us. So as I was freaking out because I was so embarrassed about my favorite Bible verse, shame was gearing up and ready to take me down. As my name was called, I took a deep breath and blurted out "John 3:16." Yes, that verse, the one that everyone knows, the one that people hold up on signs at basketball games, the most basic Bible verse there is... I said it quickly, and put my head down waiting for laughs and the wave of shame to take over, drowning me. Instead, what happened was that the woman facilitating the group leaned over to me and simply said, "Erica, tell us why."

I don't think she understood what she did in that moment, and even thinking of the small gesture today still brings tears to my eyes. She had opened the door to the next step I needed to face my shame. One of the things that we need to combat our shame is meaningful connection: we need to be around people who are worthy of hearing our story. Her saying "tell us why" in the sweet, loving, grandmotherly way she always spoke was enough to show me that I did have a seat at this table and I did belong here.

What I said to this room filled with people who had not yet heard my story, was this: when I was eight years old, I was at a private school that required us to remember Bible verses, and the first one I had to memorize was John 3:16. Since then, that verse has shown up in different parts of my life when I'm questioning my worthiness. It showed up when I was an 8-year-old who was trying to figure out life, trying to understand why these things were happening to me. I was living in this new place, my parents' divorce had been finalized, and my mother was starting a new life with a new family. Things were not OK, I was not OK, but there was no room to speak because other people's problems were bigger than mine... but that verse was a reminder that there's something greater I'm connected to, there is something else out there.

When I became a mother, that verse meant something else to me, because I knew the love of a parent to a child, and for the first time understood the magnitude of being responsible for another human being and the ultimate sacrifice that He made for me. It's hard for me to even let somebody cut in front of me at Starbucks when I'm in need of my fuel for the day. This verse was my reminder that I am a good person, that someone out there sees me as worthy, even when I don't see myself that way.

That night when the class ended, I was driving home in the rain, overwhelmed with emotion. I pulled over in the "In-N-Out Burger" parking lot and I said to myself, "This is it; I cannot do this anymore." In that moment, I said to myself that something had to die for me to live. So there in the parking lot, I had a reckoning with my shame. I'm sure the people at In-N-Out were trying to figure out what was wrong with me, as I sat in my car, crying and talking to myself. I knew that I had to put it all on the table and release what had been keeping me chained to my shame.

This is what we know when it comes to shame: shame only survives in silence, not speaking light to our shame allows it to fester and grow. I had to say the things I had been too ashamed to say out loud, I had to acknowledge the hurts in order to heal. Sitting in the car that night, basically having this "Come to Jesus" meeting with myself, I had to tell myself: "I AM WORTHY. I am worthy of having my voice heard, and worthy of speaking my truth and sharing my story."

I was ready to stop there, thinking I had done all the work and that now, finally, life would be grand. My practice was doing well, I was able to start speaking more at conferences, had taken leadership roles with organizations close to my heart, and the self-esteem and self-confidence groups I had created for young girls were selling out each round just days after being open for registration. Life was smooth sailing, or so I thought.

Being a person of faith, I have an understanding that I am called, and being called means that I will be led on a path that, at times, entails doing things I don't always understand in the moment, but that are part of a larger plan. That call, this time, was in the form of a request to get on stage and tell my story. Like most normal families, in our household when we need to make a big decision or finish a big project, we gather in the kitchen and have the biggest, loudest dance party you can imagine. Yes, full-fledged "Best of the 90's" dance party. When there have been no words, music has always been my solace. I have no musical talent; I'm a horrible dancer and I can't carry a tune, but music is in my bones. Moving and singing off-key to music always centers me. After a good dance party, I usually have a 3 a.m. *AHA!* moment, and then I can allow the creative process to flow. This 3 a.m. *AHA!* came in the form of a song called "Reckless Love." We had been playing this song on repeat after hearing it at my son's freshman retreat:

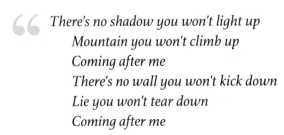

> *There's no shadow you won't light up*
> *Mountain you won't climb up*
> *Coming after me*
> *There's no wall you won't kick down*
> *Lie you won't tear down*
> *Coming after me*

Their class motto was "There is no fear in love." Those words were a reminder that I am worthy and that I am enough. Speaking my truth and telling my story was an act of love that I had been denying myself.

Stepping on that stage and sharing the pain that shame had caused me and the joy that I had found in finding the courage to face my shame meant saying goodbye to the people who had interfered in the process of me loving myself. Speaking my truth meant removing the labels that I had been carrying around for so long.

That night in the In-N-Out parking lot, I had to face every fear I've ever had about myself. I realized that the labels I had been carrying had been assigned *to me* from people and experiences that were no longer serving me. Some of those people had projected their own shame onto me when it was too heavy for them to carry alone. I had inadvertently been carrying the burdens of others, keeping myself trapped in the shame bubble.

Stepping into my power and purpose was scary; I questioned "who are these people, and can I trust them with my story? Are these people going to receive what I have to say and are they going to understand me?" Owning our power and purpose means those questions fade away. Having the courage to face our fears and having the courage to speak up and say "this is me" means that we have mastered the ability to get back up when we fall, and to keep trying. Shame will stop us from getting back up; shame tells us there's no way out and that we're stuck. We can't learn or grow or change when shame is leading us, and it gives us labels that eventually lead to us adding labels to ourselves. Standing on that stage, I declared to all that would listen who I am. I removed the labels and chose to have only one label moving forward; the only label I need at this point in my life is one that says *I am me*. I am someone who is courageous, someone who can be brave, someone who messes up but gets back up, no matter how bruised or bloody, and tries again.

There is no fear in love, and I love the person that I have embraced and the person that I am becoming. Each day I wake up, I reject shame, and I choose courage over fear.

In the G.E.M.S.® groups (Girls Empowered, Motivated and

Strong) that I created, one of my favorite activities to do is with young girls who are just starting on their journey of building their courage and facing their shame is an activity aimed at letting go of our shame story and stepping into our courageous story, learning what it means to be brave and showing up as our best self. The activity is writing our own Oriki. An Oriki is a traditional Yoruba praise poem, which translates to "praise of the head." I came across it while reading a book by Luvvi Ajayi Jones called "Professional Troublemaker." In the book, she talks about the importance of writing your Oriki to remind yourself of who you are. When my shame walks into a room with me, I repeat my own Oriki, which has become my shield of protection. I do this ritual every time I speak, no matter where I'm speaking: if I'm speaking to the girls in my G.E.M.S.® group, if I'm meeting a client for the first time, if I'm training professionals, or speaking on the corner. I start with my personal prayer, "Continue to use me as you see fit, and help guide my words for your purpose."

And then, like my favorite cartoon superhero She-Ra the Princess of Power would pull out her Sword of Protection when going to battle, I pull out my Oriki to remind myself who I am:

My name is Erica Tatum-Sheade

I am a Slayer of Shame

Navigator of Negative Thoughts

Proponent of Purpose

Holder of Healing Words

Vault for Vulnerability

Empress of Empowerment

That is who I am, and those are my fighting words, those are the words that I say to keep shame at bay when it comes to steal my voice, or tries to keep me small. When we show up as our wholehearted self and face our fears and speak into existence who we are, shame cannot exist. Shame only exists in silence. When we speak, when we use our voices and say "this is who I am," shame cannot survive. Speaking into existence who we are at our core is what moves us from just surviving into thriving.

I may not be the loudest voice in the room, but my voice is powerful, my voice has meaning, my voice is my own.

My name is Erica Tatum-Sheade, shame fighter, mother, daughter, granddaughter of queens, champion for children and adolescents, wife, the girl with no voice who found her voice. The woman who will continue to build a table for those looking for a place to sit, creating space in the world so that no one, EVER, lacks the courage to be who they are.

I am courage, I am clarity, I am confidence, and *I Am Enough*.

ERICA TATUM-SHEADE
ABOUT THE AUTHOR

Erica Tatum-Sheade is Licensed Clinical Social Worker, Registered Play Therapist™ and Certified Daring Way Facilitator™ practicing in Scottsdale Arizona. She co-owns Integrated Mental Health Associates and the Arizona Institute for Advanced Psychotherapy Training with her husband and fellow Arizona State Sun Devil. In 2018, after seeing a growing need for support for young girls, she created a group curriculum called G.E.M.S.® (Girls Empowered, Motivated, and Strong), where she teaches concepts of confidence, empowerment, self-esteem, and authenticity to girls from elementary through high school. She provides training and public speaking on mental health, shame-fighting and parenting to the public and other helping professionals. She is also the CMC (Chief Mom in Charge) in helping her family run the online clothing company FCK (Fight Confront and Knockout) The Stigma, aimed at creating conversations around mental health one shirt at a time. One of the 2021 NAWBO Arizona Woman of Vision award winners and the 2022 National Association of Social Worker-Arizona Chapter Social Worker of the Year, Erica serves her community and her purpose by advocating and volunteering for organizations she believes are doing what she calls "hearts work."

www.ericatatumsheadelcsw.com

8

YOU'VE COME A LONG WAY, LADY

By Dr. Coylette James

I stared at the pills in my hand for a very long time. I stared until they were no longer pills, but a promise. An escape hatch from a life I no longer valued.

And that's when I shoveled them into my tear-stained face, and swallowed every last one.

But I'm getting ahead of myself...

What an incredible honor it is for me to appear in this book along with the Phenomenal Women assembled here. Their stories will absolutely encourage you to be all that you have been created to be.

As I share my story, I want to give you an inside glimpse of who I am from my own perspective. So often we read about others from our view of their lives, never fully understanding who they really are or why they feel the way they do about life. I thought if I shared my assessment of my representation in the earth realm up front, you will be able to appreciate my journey to who I am at this point of life.

As a woman, I so appreciate our current standing of worth in all spheres of influence. However, I am very aware that we have not yet arrived at the true place of equality. When I was growing up, there was a particular marketing slogan that was very popular to attract the female population. It was promoted by a brand of cigarettes to entice ladies to buy and smoke them. The brand was Virginia Slims and the slogan was, "You've come a long way baby."

Now I must be transparent here and let you know that, as a teenager, I embraced this and smoked that brand of cigarettes. It spoke to the inner me to believe that, as females, we had come a long way, and to have our own specific marketing campaign was a sign of our advancement. Even if it was to partake in a habit that could cut our life short.

What I did not understand at that stage of my life was that true equality was still a very long way away.

From my perspective, equality means not needing to quantify gender, ethnicity, or spiritual beliefs. This is not the current state of being in my American Culture. For example, I am writing my first script for what I believe will be a blockbuster movie that will give women the ability to appreciate their value no matter what their past may have been. Its #1 focus is to encourage women to embrace the inner strength we possess. It tackles head-on how we as women devalue who we truly are and the greatness that dwells within us when, ultimately, we are Royalty and do not know it.

If we cannot appreciate our value as women, then we are having an identity crisis. We have been told we are too emotional, too needy, and in my case as a black woman, too angry. Corporate America has lowered our rate of pay when compared to our male counterparts, and we must work much harder for recognition for promotion. I am merely stating facts, and no, I am not a cliché angry black woman.

Back to my Blockbuster Movie script: when it is produced, released, and wins an Oscar, the headlines will focus on the fact that not only was it written by a woman, but a *black woman* at that. If we were in a true state of equality, it would be more about what an incredible movie it is, and less about the gender or ethnicity of the writer. When Chloe Zhao won her Oscar for directing Nomadland, it was a very big deal. She was the first female Asian director to ever win an Oscar. To be the first at anything is a spectacular thing. My point is, the fact that it took years upon years for an Asian Female to be in position to win shows both that we have come a long way, but also that equality is still in the process of progress. Not trying to dis anyone, but when a white male gains accolades for their work, the fact that they are white, and a man, never comes up.

Although I am no longer a somewhat naïve teenager, I still recognize and embrace the fact that we have come a very long way, but still have a ways to go to truly see equality.

The lack of true equality has a way of devaluing the "lesser" of the equal scale. Perception feeds the mindset, so if you perceive that others think less of you, quite often you will adapt to the same thoughts about yourself.

FULFILLING PURPOSE

One of my assignments or purposes in life is to help others recognize the greatness within them. To be honest, it is my true passion to help women understand that their value is more precious than gold. We are more than eye candy for someone to show off. While I love to look pretty as much as the next woman, I know and hope to relay to others that our value is not in our looks (which, by the way, keep changing). Your value was established at your creation. I am not talking about when your mother and father engaged in a sexual act. Your creation came way before that in the mind of God. Your parents were the catalysts to bring you forth. You were created on purpose, for a purpose. It is not by accident that you are alive in this time sphere. You are the answer to a need in this world, more importantly in the life of others.

Let me tell you something that I wish someone had told me before I woke up one night regurgitating all over myself because, before I laid down, I had taken that handful of pills: YOU ARE NOT A MISTAKE! YOU ARE NOT UNWORTHY!

By my early twenties I had been told some of the foulest things about my existence and one day I had enough. I was my mother's caregiver and had two small children. Having been given up for adoption at birth and then birthing two children myself by 16, life had been challenging. What I did not realize, and had to come to terms with, was that even though my circumstances in life hadn't been ideal, that did not diminish my value.

For those of you who may have had a rocky start in life or maybe just heard one too many negative things spoken about you, it is vital to come face to face with the truth of our surrounding culture and understand: we are not the sum of what others may say or think about us. Something may have been said to you as a child, either directly or in passing, that still plays repeatedly in your mind, and because of that, you may think yourself less than who you really are.

Let me say this now, and I pray you receive it deep down in your Spirit: YOU WERE CREATED WITH GREATNESS WITHIN YOU TO ACCOMPLISH MONUMENTAL THINGS IN LIFE! When you embrace this, life will take on new meaning. It will not cause you to be caught up in vainglory or pride. Quite the contrary, when you realize the enormity of your contribution to those around you, it is very humbling. You will begin to be extremely mindful of everyone you encounter and the need to leave them in a better place than before they met you.

CURRENT STAGE OF LIFE

I am 66 Years old, and at this stage of life, am truly very comfortable in my own skin. By some accounts I would be considered somewhat successful. Worked for 28 years for a world-renowned personality which afforded me the opportunity to travel the globe working on historical sporting events. Second in charge of the multimillion-dollar small business I work for now. Have published three books of my own and one compilation with two more in the works. Have been married to the same man for the past 33 years. I share my story on Global stages and am blessed to help others identify the greatness which resides within them. Pretty fair to say God has been good to me.

To say that I am unapologetically me would sum up my current state of being. This has not always been the case, as shared earlier. So glad now that I threw the pills up, because I would have truly hated to have missed the last 40 plus years of life because of all the issues in the first 20.

If you don't mind, I would like to take you on a time in reverse journey to give you a little deeper inside view of my beginnings. This is not a fairy tale, so it won't begin with once upon a time. It is more like, what had happened was – which, for those not in-the-know, is the urban translation for once upon a time.

MY HISTORY

Born in 1956 in San Francisco, CA. to an unwed mother who had been put out of her aunt's house because of her "condition" and the stigma surrounding it. My mother thought it best to go to a home for unwed mothers and placed me up for adoption.

Please note here, from my perspective, this was not a bad decision. I am grateful that she chose to give me life and not the alternative. In honesty, I look back on my introduction to this earth realm with joy. How you perceive situations you have lived through will shape how you handle things to come. Keep in mind, it's never too late to change your perception. I have friends who were adopted by very loving people however, they never got past the feeling of rejection in their life. They carry this dark cloud with them everywhere they go. Something insignificant from someone else's viewpoint will immediately be perceived as rejection by them. I choose to look at adoption not as rejection but as being specially assigned to people handpicked by God. What an honor to be the answer to someone's prayers before you even know what prayer is.

My Mother was from New Orleans and was in San Francisco to further her education. She was charmed by this tall 6'8" tall, handsome man who basically swept her off her feet. Although she was in her early twenties, there was still that streak of naivety in her as her religious parents kept her pretty sheltered. Though I was not wanted by my sperm donor, nor the only family my mother had in Cali at the time, I did not grow up in the hardship of being tossed from foster home to foster home. I was adopted at 3 months old by a very loving middle-aged couple.

As far back as I can remember, I carried within me a dream of someday meeting my biological mother and letting her know how much I loved and appreciated her even though I didn't know her. I wanted her to know that what she did was a good thing. Unfortunately, I never got that chance. I searched for her for many years, but not knowing her name hindered me from uncovering her identity while she was alive. I did, however, find out who she was last year, which allowed me to get some answers regarding my lineage.

To say that my first 7 years on this planet were great would be accurate. My Father was a wonderful man who instilled family values into me by example. Yes, I was that classic Daddy's little girl. He was my world. My mother owned a beauty salon, and my parents together owned a small 6-unit apartment complex along with a 5-unit store front building. They were what would be considered a middle-class black family. I only mention their race here because, considering the climate of racial tension in the 50s & 60s in America, I am very proud of their accomplishments. One of the things I applaud them for is the fact that in the midst of the racial climate of that era, I never heard them discuss race in front of me. They never pointed the finger at any ethnicity to blame them for anything. I was taught that I could accomplish anything in life I wanted. Just keep working toward it, and it will happen. This is a life lesson that I still live by today.

They did not come from wealthy ancestry, nor were they wealthy in their own right. What they were was a hard-working couple who were never in competition with each other. Instead, they worked together to build a comfortable life for their family. My father was a presser in a downtown dry cleaner, and my mother a cosmetologist.

Both had previous failed marriages. My father had married very young, either late teens or early twenties, because he had impregnated someone. This marriage would last only for a couple of years. Born in 1909, he lived through some trying times in Texas. The third born of 9 children to sharecropper parents, there was always a shortage of everything growing up.

My mother, who was born in 1913 in Ft. Smith Arkansas, had lived in Phoenix Arizona as an adolescent and later moved to Los Angeles California for almost 20 years before moving to Las Vegas. She had been married twice before my father. She, too, had lived a hard life prior to finding love and actual happiness.

They both found themselves in Las Vegas due to the building of the Hoover Dam in the 1940s. My Father came to work on the dam and my mother used to drive back and forth from Los Angeles to do hair because, at that time, Las Vegas was still a little dirt town, and a beautician for the black population was a rarity.

They were total opposites. She was very flighty and fiery. When she got angry, everybody knew it. While she was the epitome of grace and elegance, if you made her mad, she could cuss you out so profusely it would make a sailor blush. Never one to hold back her opinion, she was not afraid to throw a temper tantrum from time to time. He was soft-spoken; in fact, I don't believe I ever heard him raise his voice. I won't say he never got angry, but he had to really be pushed to show it. He was her balance; the only person on the planet that could calm her down.

Why have I gone into such detail about my parents? It is only because of who they were in my life that I am who I am. You can learn a lot about who someone is now when you understand where they come from. My Father taught me the importance of honor and the love of family. We were his top priority. He instilled Godly values as well: we went to church every Sunday as a family. And the same people they were in church were the same people they were at home. He gave me his name and never treated me as anything less than his daughter whom he loved as if I came out of his loins. My mother taught me how to be a STRONG woman of Grace & Class. I emphasize strong because her strength was one of the most intriguing things about her.

I mentioned earlier that the first seven years of my life were great. At age 7, my father died from leukemia. It rocked my world. He was my sunshine, moon and all the stars rolled up in one. Not to say that I didn't love my mother, but she worked very long hours in the salon, so most of my non-school time was spent with my father. The shop was closed on Sunday and Monday, so that was family time. During the week, though, it was me and daddy time. My grandfather lived with us too, so when my father wasn't there, it was his leg I swung on as my horsey.

There is no doubt losing her husband had a profound effect on my mother as well. However, she didn't miss a beat. We went to see him before the public was allowed to, and my mother was her normal, no-mess self. When she saw him, she went off. The makeup they put on him was darker than his natural skin tone. She told them her husband had never been that dark in his life and they were going to have to take him back and redo him. She told them not to get any of the makeup on his shirt because she was not bringing another one up there for them to cut up the back. She also told the mortician to open the coffin all the way because she wanted to make sure they put all his clothes on, including his socks.

I didn't understand at such a young age that this was part of her coping method. She had to be totally in control and on top of everything to get through it. At the funeral, she may have shed a couple of tears, but not many; she was watching everyone else around her. Within two months of my father passing, my grandfather trimmed a toe and it got infected and his leg had to be amputated. He never made it back home after surgery. My mother lost her husband and father two months apart, out of the same house, and once again, it was all about her incredible resolve to just handle it and keep going that I saw demonstrated before me.

All my life I have been told how strong I am, and I want to tell people who my mother was, therefore I had no choice but to be strong. She demanded nothing less. In my teens, we were having one of our many heated discussions, and I reminded her that she raised me to be independent and her reply was "yes, of everybody but me." I said it didn't work that way: either I was going to be dependent or independent, and she looked at me like I had two heads. In her mind there was never a question of her role in my life, no matter how much she taught me not to rely on others for anything I wanted.

I am truly grateful for her life lessons. She never allowed me to make excuses, no matter what was going on in society. She would tell me I could achieve anything in life that I wanted. I may have to work harder and longer than some to do it, but I could do it. She instilled a tenacious work ethic within me. Honestly, I have had to work hard the past few years to balance my personal life with my work life because I have been a workaholic most of my life. As they say, children learn by example.

HOW OUR PAST CAN DEFINE US

Now what I just shared with you is a little snippet of my life history. Besides the fact that my parents are the heroes of my life story, there is another reason why I shared all of this with you. When you read the beginning of this chapter and I told you about my challenges, all you could see was the dark side of my life. Now that I have shared what wonderful loving parents I had, you may stop and think, my life really wasn't all that bad.

If you had been around back when I had my first child at 14 and then my second child at 16, you might have been one of the people saying unpleasant things about me. Again, it's all about perception. You would think how blessed I was to have been adopted at 3 months old and not grown up in foster care, was in private school from the 2nd to the 8th grade, and was thought to have had a somewhat privileged life within the neighborhood. Even with the birth of both my children, I graduated from high school right on schedule, thanks to the help of my mother. She would take the kids to work with her during the day since it was her salon. I can remember a time when she had a crib sitting right in the middle of the shop, and that was where they were.

Whether you are looking at my life from the dark side or the good side, you still are only seeing snippets of my past or who I truly am. When people judge you, they don't know all of you, most don't even know the real you, only what you have chosen to share. This is why it is so important to not allow what they say or how they react to you to govern your self-perception. There is so much to my story that you have no idea about, and which truly won't fit in this one chapter. The same is true about you. You have the inside scoop on your life, you have the power to choose how you see yourself. Stop giving that power away!

MY STRUGGLE FOR MY VALUE

My struggle with my value started at age 13 when I lost my virginity. That was something very precious to me. I envisioned myself walking down the aisle on my wedding day with a white veil over my face, signifying my purity. When I allowed someone to take that from me, my value of myself went with it. Then when I had my children, people said all sorts of foul and negative things about me. I developed a thick skin very quickly. However, even though I said I didn't care what they said or thought about me, my treatment of myself said something very different. I became very promiscuous.

My teens were consumed with school, work, and taking care of my children. I missed most of the things young adolescents enjoyed. But it was just what I was conditioned to do. Whatever the situation, just push through it and "be strong." Let me tell you, strength has its place, but it can also cost you. What my mother silently taught me without ever saying it is that when you continually just suck it up, after a while, it's going to come out in some form or fashion.

For my mother, it was alcohol; for me, it was drugs. By the time I was 20, I had two failed relationships, neither of which was with my children's fathers, which just added to the feeling of nothingness. The drugs became my outlet and release. Even after the failed suicide attempt, I changed a little, but was still trying to self-medicate the void that I felt inside. That void was my value of who I was.

This lifestyle continued until I turned 32 and decided to seek a different path in life. My spiritual connection and relationship with God were my redemption. Now, 34 years later, I am so grateful for that fork in the road and choosing to walk a higher path in life. I don't know what your fork in the road will be, but I do know it will come to a choice you will have to make to see something greater in you in order to embrace the true value you are to everyone around you.

If you haven't yet learned to appreciate you for you, it is time to look at the person you see in the mirror and determine whether you like them. If not, then change who you see. If you do, then embrace them and live your life to the fullest. No matter where you started in life or what you have encountered on your journey through life, know this: You *have* come a long way, baby!

DR. COYLETTE JAMES

A highly driven woman who was born to break barriers, Dr. Coylette James proves that when powered by purpose, women are unstoppable.

She's built her career brick by brick, fighting fears, failures, and setbacks to have the success she's always known was hers to claim. Coming from a past that included being given away at birth, two teenage pregnancies, drug use, and many other trials, Dr. Coylette has a passion for helping others overcome past difficulties.

Today she personifies what it means to ascend above adversity while inspiring countless others to do the same.

Having honed her expertise for over a decade, her work is a testament to what it means to leave an undeniable mark on the world.

She inspires. She empowers. She unleashes.

Extraordinary at walking others through radical transformation, she is as relentless about her clients' success as she is her own.

She doesn't simply change lives – she expands them.

www.linktr.ee/drcoylette

ABOUT WOMEN THRIVE MEDIA

WOMEN
THRIVE
MEDIA

Women Thrive Media - Women Thrive is a global media platform where every woman has a voice. Where every woman's story is celebrated. We recognise the impact and contribution that women make in the world, and our mission is to build a platform where every woman feels included, celebrated and proud to be part of a community like this.

We started our mission work in 2017 and have since grown to an international platform of over 600k women worldwide. Over the years, we have hosted many amazing and life-changing events, had

100's inspiring international speakers take our stage, and thousands of attendees' lives changed or impacted by our work.

Now we pride ourselves on being an inclusive platform where women looking for guidance, support and mentorship can come and connect with others who have already walked the walk and share their knowledge and wisdom. Be it through our podcast, events, book, or monthly Women Thrive magazine.

Our mission is to reach one million women every year and create a global impact on women's empowerment because we believe that if one woman is given the confidence, tools and resources to rise, she will go on to empower thousands more. We have seen time and time again when we, as women, come together, the impact and ripple effect is so much more powerful than a woman trying to make an impact on her own.

We hope you join our community, mission, and future events.

www.womenthrivesummit.com
www.womenthrivemagazine.com

THANK YOU

If you found this book helpful, we would greatly appreciate a simple review on

    Amazon amzn.to/3YUFq5R
    or **GoodReads.**

PUBLISHER'S NOTE

The contributing authors of this anthology are from countries around the world. As such, we have elected to retain the authors' voice by using the preferred spellings from each country.

Printed in Great Britain
by Amazon

38575676R00078